Total Indifference

How America Chooses Guns Over People

By Michael M. Nunes

Dedicated to the innocent children who lost their lives in the Sandy Hook Elementary School massacre in Newtown, Connecticut, and to the brave and selfless teachers who gave their lives trying to save their young charges.

To the victims of the mass shootings in the Pulse nightclub in Orlando, Las Vegas, Umpqua Community College, San Bernadino, Sutherland Springs Church, and Douglas High School.

To the unknown victims of gun violence, and to the people who fight daily for their right to life over the right to own firearms.

Contents

Preface

The gun lobby and its proponents often claim that guns do not kill, people kill. The reality is that guns do not solve problems, people solve problems. The gun lobby uses firearms to attempt to solve every societal ill, but it is only when people cooperate, compromise and work together that we solve our problems.

The gun debate is not so much a debate as it is a false display of masculine bravado, a way to shout down an opponent using a facade of legal authority. The lives lost, the brutality visited upon some segments of the population, the children taken too early, and the women intimidated, assaulted, injured or killed, seldom feature in the debate. Much of the debate revolves around the putative right to carry firearms, rather than an attempt to mitigate the fatalities and injuries that invariably result from the presence of firearms. Few discussions outside the research community forcefully expose the heartrending impact of firearm possession on families, on society and on communities such as the mentally ill, who have little to do with gun violence.

The terrible tragedy that shook this nation with the massacre in Newtown, Connecticut did not inspire America to end the firearm cult; rather it fueled an unprecedented drive for increased access to destructive armaments. Tragedies of this magnitude have driven other nations to reevaluate the rationale behind the possession and access to firearms, and to restrict that access, with a predictable decline in gunfire deaths.

I dedicate this book in part to those twenty brave little souls in Newtown that gave their lives in sacrifice to our gun cult, to those wonderful teachers that tried so hard to protect their innocent charges, some of whom gave their lives for those children. I also dedicate this book to young Trayvon Martin, who was cut down in his prime. The man who took his life escaped the consequences of his actions by claiming that he felt threatened by a teenager armed only with skittles and iced tea. The nations' youth should not be forced to suffer under the irrational obsession with extreme weapons.

I have borrowed shamelessly from newspaper articles and scientific studies, from opinions given by the public in on-line journals, from lists of pro-gun and gun-control perspectives. I thank those journalists who spent time researching so that I did not have to, scientists who labored to collect data, to those who gave opinions, and to those who stoked my anger, my emotions and my reason.

In particular, I thank experts in the field, such as Prof. David Hemenway, whose tireless work exposing the misconceptions and fallacies of the gun industry provided many of the ideas and facts around which this book took shape. The data available from gunpolicy.org[1] was particularly helpful, as was the study conducted by motherjones.com[2] into mass shootings. The United Nations Small Arms Survey was particularly enlightening in its valiant attempts to fight the international arms trade against the lobbying of the well-funded arms industry. It is a great shame that gunpolicy.org has now ceased operation; their website was an invaluable research tool.

I have done my best to be factual and to provide reference to relevant facts, where possible. As for my opinion, I make no apologies for my ardent anti-gun stance. I have heard no compelling argument yet that would persuade me that a nation or the planet without guns would not be a far better place than one plagued by guns, hunters and the arms industry. Humans can, and should, live without guns and the terrible death and destruction that accompany them. As an advanced people and civilization, we should be able to compromise on our differences in a rational, thoughtful manner through the judicial and legislative process rather than resolving them with arrogance and violence.

Much of the research cited in this book originates in the 1990's, especially the early 1990's. While most non-fiction requires current data, the gun lobby has been successful in preventing researchers, especially government researchers, and organizations like the FBI, from doing research into the causes of gun violence. This intellectual obstructionism only serves to mask an extreme gun agenda and does nothing to mitigate the ongoing gun-related death toll in the United States. However, much of the research done in the 1990's is still relevant, as certain statistical ratios seldom change in any serious way, given a similar set of circumstances. It would be far more honest, and demonstrate intellectual integrity to allow intensive research into the causes and solutions for gun violence. It is a testament to President Barack Obama's foresight that he issued a Presidential order permitting the CDC to continue research into gun violence.

Regardless of the paucity of research into gun violence, what research exists is clear; nations with more firearms have more gun deaths from all causes than those with fewer. It is not difficult to ascertain the cause.

Preface to Revised Edition

Five years have elapsed since the massacre of 20 children and 6 teachers in the Sandy Hook Elementary School, in Newtown, Connecticut. For all the anger, the demonstrations, the vigils, and the demands for action, nothing has changed. Red states have loosened gun restrictions. The firearm death toll continues its ominous rise.

On the afternoon of February 14th, 2018, a 19 year-old former student of the Marjory Stoneman Douglas High School in Parkland Florida took the lives of 17 people, including students and teachers.

The same stale arguments from gun proponents followed the shooting. It is clear from these arguments that the lives of children have less value than firearms. I despair for the continued decline in public discourse in the United States, and the ability to solve simple problems. I have come to believe that the only remedy for these continued acts of senseless violence is to make it close to impossible to own any firearm.

The battle to severely restrict or even eliminate public firearm ownership will be long and hard. In the current political and social climate, it appears impossible. The United States has solved social problems before. To overcome apathy and indifference to suffering will take sustained protest action on multiple fronts.

Yet, to succeed, we must fight for every dogged yard. The opposition is tireless in its zeal for gun ownership. Despite this, we will ultimately prevail.

Introduction

Throughout this book I use the term "gun lobby" to refer to groups representing the interests of the firearm industry, whether it is Remington, Smith and Wesson, Bushmaster or any of the gun manufacturers. These lobby groups include the NRA (National Rifle Association), GOA (Gun Owners of America), NSSF (National Shooting Sports Foundation) and dozens of smaller groups from various states. In order to avoid repetition, I include in the gun lobby those members of Congress that in effect represent the gun industry. Where applicable, I refer to the NRA or other gun groups by name. I do not see groups like the NRA as representing the real interests of gun owners, or of the public in any definitive sense. I believe that these groups constitute a cabal of special interests that has no real interest in safety, security or self-defense. They are devoted instead to power, profit, and their own narrow self-interest, regardless of the deadly consequences to society.

Variously the book examines the impact of firearms on families, especially women and children, the ubiquitous availability of firearms and their cost to us all. It also examines the inordinate costs of gun violence to the nation.

What astonished me as I researched this book was the almost complete lack of empirical evidence in favor of the private ownership of firearms. While such writers as John Lott and Gary Kleck have written against measures to mitigate gun violence, very few statistically or scientifically compelling studies are produced arguing against sensible gun restrictions. The data, such as they are, given the gun lobby's unethical fight against firearm research, argue persuasively in favor of gun limitations. Yet, there are few, if any books that cover the compelling arguments and evidence in favor of gun restrictions. I will attempt to address that need.

As with so many debates in the United States, from Climate Change and Environmental degradation to Evolution and Women's rights, conservatives, in this case the gun lobby, use emotional appeals to nationalism, tradition and a perverse interpretation of the Second Amendment to argue their case rather than cold, hard fact. To a significant extent, they are winning that argument, through threat, appeals to fear, lobbying power, financial muscle and reliance on a population often blissfully ignorant of the facts. We cannot continue, as a civilized nation, to countenance the terrible drumbeat of death and injury by gunfire.

A troubling tendency is to blame gun violence on those with mental illness, or as one commentator put it, the mentally deranged. The most frightening aspect of gun violence is that most of it is perpetrated not by those with mental illness, but by those who are from all outward appearances mostly normal. Far too much violence is driven by human emotion, by anger, resentment, or an artificially induced fear of some segment of society, all too often young black men. A lack of empathy and contempt for life are more likely to blame for gun violence than mental illness.

Even proponents of gun restrictions excuse rifles, shotguns and shooting sports without seeming to comprehend the link between all firearms and gun violence. The unnecessary taking of any life, human or animal needs to be seen through the same lens. The wanton destruction of our wild heritage is no less important than the breakdown of our communities because of gun violence.

What is striking and mystifying in the debate over gun limitations is the lack of demand for firm action by the American people. People die at a horrifying rate each day, yet people cling to their guns, ignoring the evidence that possessing a firearm is far more dangerous to a household than not owning one. This creates a more dangerous society than is necessary.

When President Obama wanted to prevent the Syrians from using chemical weapons, an appallingly inhumane weapon, the American people were outraged that more Syrians would die because of American bombing. Yet, each day in the U.S., 106 people die by gun with almost triple that number seriously injured; yet, there is no similar outrage from the American people. Assad's chemical weapons killed 426 children; in the U.S. in 2010, 571 children died through gun violence, 325 through homicide[3]. The difference between the Syrian conflict and gun deaths in the U.S. is that someday, the Syrian conflict will end; in the United States, gun deaths never end. America is reluctant to acknowledge the moral equivalence between death by weapons of mass destruction and death by ubiquitous firearms.

The staggering number of deaths each year in the United States is indicative of civil conflict or low-level civil war. A similar number of people died in the U.S. between 2009 and 2012 as died in the Syrian conflict over a comparable period, and yet Congress has effectively abrogated its responsibility and moral obligation to act to stop the violence. The need for possession of assault weapons by civilians is also emblematic of civil strife, including civil war. U.S. civilians collect personal arsenals with thousands of rounds of ammunition, and dozens of weapons as though in preparation for the threat of non-existent war, in contrast to all other developed nations, which have introduced sensible gun restrictions.

The right to possession of firearms has nothing to do with freedom, liberty, self-worth or God and country. People in countries with strict limits on firearms are as loyal to their nations, but they choose to express that loyalty through adherence to democratic norms and fairness rather than through violent responses to solvable problems. A man faced with an armed assailant is not freer if he is compelled to defend himself with a firearm; he is free when the threat of such a confrontation is almost non-existent and he has no need to own a firearm for protection. This is the case in every developed nation other than the United States.

It is only when we as a nation realize that solutions to societies problems do not proceed from the barrel of a gun, that disagreements can be resolved in a civilized and orderly fashion, that we will terminate our addiction to firearms. Most other developed nations have already arrived at that conclusion; it is time for us to catch up with them and act in a manner concordant with rational thought.

The Case for Gun Regulation

"We choose to go to the moon in this decade and to do these other things not because they are easy, but because they are hard. Because that goal will serve to organize and measure the best of our energies and skills, because that challenge is one that we are willing to accept, one we are unwilling to postpone, and one which we intend to win" **President John F Kennedy, 1962**

Bullets cannot be recalled. They cannot be uninvented. But they can be taken out of the gun **(Martin Amis)**

Impossible Restrictions

Prof. James B. Jacobs of the New York University School of Law, states[4]

> "In a country in which there are 300 million guns in civilian hands" and "the large majority of firearms used in crimes are either stolen or purchased on the black market", "is it realistic to pursue a strategy of enhanced regulation of firearms?"

In 1994, during the transition from apartheid, South Africa experienced 26,000 deaths by firearm, due largely to the weapons left over from the guerilla war against the white government. The country did not throw up their hands in capitulation over this seemingly unmanageable problem; they acted decisively to change that tragedy. Nations act when they are deep in crisis as the United States is; they cannot wait for fair weather to react. This nation has faced far more intractable problems than firearms, and we managed to resolve them. To say that we cannot succeed in ridding the nation of firearms is to surrender our fate to violence.

Both Prof Jacobs, and Prof. David Kairys of Temple University concede that[5]

> "the handgun debate at its core is related to a personal, cultural and political identification of guns with personal self worth...freedom, liberty, and ... God and country"

Western Civilization has gone through phases in which it has identified with a great many failed policies, including slavery, racism, and religious intolerance. The essential strength of the Western experiment is that it is able to overcome seemingly overwhelming odds to shed society of basic violations of human and civil rights. The gun debate by contrast is a thorn in our sides, something that may be painful to extract, but not impossible. This ought to be a debate about the sanctity of life superseding the right to own firearms, the proximate cause of so much death and debilitating injury in the United States and around the globe.

The people of the United States need to stop hiding behind a poorly crafted and misunderstood Second Amendment and craft a policy that respects the right of people to be secure in their persons without the need to possess highly destructive weapons. We should not be expected to provide for our own defense - that is the *raison d'etre* for civilized society. We do not provide all of our own food, electricity, water, clothing, medical care, roads, or construction; we rely on those around us to do many of those things for us. This is commonly known as the division of labor. As society becomes more complex, labor becomes far more specialized. This is why we employ law enforcement officers, to ensure our safety and security; we do not expect questionable and untrained vigilantes to do that job for us.

Prof. Jacobs also claims that any attempt to prohibit firearms would polarize the American population[6], but the population is already polarized on this issue. When the population comes to understand the massive cost paid by society in lives and money to support gun rights, reasonable attempts will be made to restrict access to firearms. It has never been a matter of prohibiting firearms; even one of the most restrictive nations on Earth, Japan, has some firearm ownership; it has always been about restricting how many and what types of firearms any single owner may have, how much ammunition he may store, where he may carry his firearm and where he may fire it. It is also a matter of restricting when it can be used, and under which circumstances he may be charged with a crime.

Critics often conjure a false equivalence between prohibitions on drugs, alcohol and firearms[7]. Gun restrictions can be introduced through mandatory training and licensing, firearm insurance, taxes on ammunition, firearms and gun ranges, limitations on ammunition purchases, the introduction of trigger locks and other smart technologies, funding the ATF, cracking down on gang activity and a host of other measures that do not entail confiscation. The drug war would be more effectively resolved through limiting sales to people under controlled conditions, than through either outright prohibition or legalization. The same techniques can be used to restrict firearms, as they are successfully used in Switzerland.

Many make the claim that some people would be unwilling to comply with firearm prohibitions as they do with homicide, assault and robbery. That does not stop any society from producing prohibitions against all those things. The belief that our government would be unable to enforce restrictions on some aspect of society undercuts the legitimacy of democracy and raises a far more sinister specter than gun regulation; what would a society without effective governance look like?

Sensible restrictions on firearms are essential to the maintenance of order in society. Firearms are poorly regulated in comparison with many everyday objects. Gun restrictions are never realistically designed to stop every gun crime, just to reduce those crimes to a more manageable level. Absolute control is never the result of any set of laws, even the most draconian. For any society to abdicate its primary responsibility to security is to create anarchy.

The claim is also made that Prohibition would spawn a flourishing black market in firearms. Restrictions would decrease the supply of legitimate firearms, which in turn would reduce the supply of illicit firearms, resulting in rising black market prices for those firearms and putting them out of reach of the common criminal. The very ubiquity of firearms in American society makes cheap, reliable handguns readily available to criminal elements. It makes no economic sense to any criminal to have to spend a thousand dollars on a handgun to rob a store for a few hundred.

The net result of restrictions on firearms, as in other nations, is a reduction in gun crimes. Contrary to Prof. Jacobs claims that there is a black market in firearms in a country like Japan[8], no significant market exists in that nation[9]. The net result is that in Japan gun deaths are rare. The internal trafficking of firearms in the United States is very efficient and increases street crime in New York City because of firearms available in states like Virginia. Also contrary to the professor's claims, while there may be some trafficking in European and Far Eastern countries, it is difficult to obtain firearms, resulting in lower rates of gun crime, death and injury.

Claims are also made that the gun control debate keeps shifting, and that proponents favor different controls to achieve their goals. As with the significant reduction in motor vehicle deaths over three decades, a multi-faceted approach to reductions is likely to work best, with all options being used to achieve a reduction in gun deaths.

Gun owners are not the enemy; rather it is gun violence, with its resultant death and injury that is the enemy, and society must cooperate to combat the problem. It can work as it has in other countries. We need to realize that owning a firearm does not make us free, freedom is enshrined in our democracy, our free speech, our ability to practice our religion, our freedom from slavery, coercion or indentured labor. Firearms are no guarantee of any of those things, and may be used by excessively well-armed non-state actors to compel a free people to give up those rights.

Gun Regulation Works

The available data on gun regulations are unequivocal; those developed nations with gun restrictions have fewer guns, and fewer gun deaths and injuries. Gun crimes, or those instances in which guns are used in crimes, are lower in those countries with gun restrictions. Some may dispute this, but one need only examine those nations to appreciate the truth. The same dynamic is at work within the United States; in those states with strict legislation, there are fewer guns, and fewer deaths and injuries, in comparison to those states with lenient gun laws and many guns. The gun lobby has convinced Americans that gun regulations do not work in stark contrast to the disheartening reality that more guns make us far less safe than other developed nations.

In countries that have introduced gun regulation, like South Africa and Brazil, both of which have high gun deaths, the results have been staggeringly successful, with homicides, gun crimes, accidental deaths and suicides all declining. The gun lobby leads a campaign of disinformation, bad science, political corruption and scientific obstructionism to lead gullible voters into believing that gun restrictions do not work, and that society should have more guns than it already does.

Lobbyists and organizations that argue that gun regulations do not work must show data from a wide variety of sources to conclusively demonstrate that they do not work. Unfortunately, the pro-gun lobby make claims that are not substantiated without cherry-picking from the data.

As with any set of laws or regulations, sensible societies put the safety of their citizens above ideological absolutism, above religious documents or texts, and above the desires of small but vocal special interests within that society. The US Constitution has many limitations, and the Second Amendment, like all the other amendments, is no different.

The Regulation Debate

The irony is that it was tougher to rent a car from Cerberus when it owned Alamo than to buy a semi-automatic. To rent a car, one had to provide ID, a driver's license and get insurance coverage. To buy a gun? Cash and carry from the back of a station wagon at a gun show. No concerns about downstream liability or risk ***(Eliot Spitzer)***

Opponents of gun control sometimes claim that proponents believe that guns are inherently evil and cause crime, homicide, suicide and accidents. Guns are not evil, they are ultimately inert metallic objects; it is what they enable people to do with greater ease than they would otherwise be able to do that is at issue. People and guns together are a lethal combination, and as such, we need to regulate access to firearms.

Gun proponents claim that where there are gun restrictions, there is confiscation, and that does not accord with the facts. Whereas in war-torn areas of the world, the disarming of the combatants is essential to the restoration of peace and political stability, in developed countries, gun ownership is often quite common. However, in most developed nations there are strict controls on the use of those weapons, as well there should be. Additionally, the ownership rates are almost all less than a third lower than those in the United States are. However, ownership is not the only predictor of deaths and injuries; the availability of ammunition and the rules governing firearm use are just as important in determining injury and fatality. The results of restrictive gun policies in developed nations have shown astonishing success at reducing gun death and injuries.

In the United States, there is still much debate as to whether gun regulation would be effective at reducing gun violence. In much of the rest of the developed world, that argument has been settled by appeal to empirical data. The firearm injury rate in those nations is extremely low in comparison to the United States. In the United States, the increasingly powerful gun lobby has successfully framed the debate, by ignoring, discounting or disparaging the evidence that gun restriction works.

Despite the refusal of Congress to consider legislation controlling gun violence, resulting in weakened gun laws rather than strengthened laws, there is some room for hope. GE Capital, based in Fairfield, Connecticut withdrew loans for firearms after the massacre in Newtown, Connecticut[10]. They are one of a number of financial institutions that have taken this step. Cerberus Capital will divest itself of Freedom Group, which manufactures the Bushmaster used in the Newtown shooting.

It remains to be seen whether these companies will retain this stance or not. In December 2013, a year after the Newtown shooting, Cerberus still appeared to own the Freedom Group, based on the latter's third quarter 2013 financial report. With gun companies reaping record profits in the wake of the Newtown massacre, there is no reason for them to sell. The actions of Cerberus increasingly sound like another marketing ploy to attract gullible customers. It should not take the massacre of elementary school children to force change on the nations gun culture.

The 2008 Supreme Court was the first to affirm an individual right to keep and bear arms for self-defense[11]. Cases brought before the high court in the seven decades before that date held no such right and affirmed only a militia's right to bear arms. This argument is still misunderstood by many Americans who believe that this right has always been held by the Court.

The gun lobby attempts to use the wording of the Second Amendment and others to contend that Congress can do absolutely nothing to regulate the possession of firearms. They have missed the point of restrictions on firearms; that they are intended to make for a safer society. Insisting on a right in the face of the harm that it does to society is not a rational choice to make. Any Constitution is only as good as the society that it produces. The Second Amendment has not produced a safer society; rather it is dramatically less safe for everyone.

Gun Prohibition

The gun lobby often claims that any attempt to regulate firearms will lead to a slippery slope of cascading gun laws intended to tear every firearm from its owner's arms. Laws to regulate motor vehicles have not led to a cascade of restrictive laws, nor have they led to confiscation. Laws regulating teddy bears and water pistols have not led in that direction either. We have an expansive legislative canon that regulates almost every facet of our lives, and those laws for the most part do not circumscribe our freedom. If anything, they create more freedom by implementing a set of rules that is supposed to make it fairer for all participants in our market economy. The firearm industry is the only industry that is not regulated to any significant extent, and the result is a disastrous spiral of death and injury. We need sufficiently strict gun laws to ensure that the death rate declines dramatically along with the injury rate, and no more.

The claim that gun regulation will lead inexorably to a total ban and confiscation need not be the case. Numerous measures to prevent gun violence do not require confiscation. James B. Jacobs of New York University talked of Prohibition and the disaster of that policy[12]. He claims by this that since history shows that prohibitions are disastrous, that we should not even try to implement such laws. The fact is that society introduces a great number of prohibitions, many of which people disobey. That is an essential part of the legislative process. If society stopped producing legislation to regulate, modify or control social behaviors, civil society would disintegrate, leading to catastrophic lawlessness and social collapse.

While few advocate a total prohibition of firearms, if we were to implement such a policy, we would do it because it is the right thing to do, even if it is hard to do, as President John F. Kennedy said of the moon landings. People cannot claim that restricting access to firearms is too hard, and that therefore we should not try. The alternative is clearly to allow the current unacceptably high death rate to continue unabated. It implicitly accepts the danger of being killed by a firearm as an acceptable byproduct of gun possession. If there are ways to reduce gun violence even marginally, it is incumbent upon us as a society to do so.

One argument by the gun lobby is that while during Prohibition liquor needed replenishing, a single firearm purchase can last a lifetime and is therefore harder to regulate. Perhaps that is true, but ammunition does not last, it does deteriorate and needs to be replaced, and restricting or removing the supply of ammunition is a simple way to regulate firearms without taking them away. Weapons also rust, need to be repaired, and parts replaced; if those repairs are no longer available, the firearm is worthless. Additionally, if firearms, or certain firearms were no longer available, the number of those weapons would gradually decline, leaving fewer in homes and fewer in the hands of undesirable elements.

I do not believe that a campaign of enforcement against gun possession in the event of Prohibition of firearms, or certain firearms, is necessary. Merely restricting firearms and ammunition purchases and introducing laws concerning the private use of firearms would suffice to reduce the deadly toll of firearm deaths. These restrictions have worked spectacularly well in Japan, possibly the world's most law-abiding nation, and would work here. The law-abiding citizen would obey these laws; the alternative is a criminal act. We cannot claim that gun owners are law abiding and in the same breath say that in the event of Prohibition, those same people will disobey the law.

We cannot choose which laws to obey, we may fight laws we feel are unjust, but we cannot choose to ignore them. The gun lobby also hides behind insidiously crafted laws that it has created through its sycophants in Congress. We also cannot grant immunity to law breakers by saying that otherwise law abiding citizens would get guns on the black market, any more than we can speak of otherwise law abiding murderers, rapists or robbers.

Self-Defense

The assumption implicit in gun ownership is that firearms provide personal protection to the owner and his family. This is almost routinely assumed by all sides in the gun debate. Yet, the evidence shows clearly that firearms are more dangerous to the owner and his family than not having firearms. Firearms are far more likely to be used as an instrument that endangers the lives of those surrounding the owner.

Claims that gun possessors are motivated by anxiety about personal security, an ideological belief in the right to firearms, the enjoyment of hunting and target shooting and criminal intent, which will prevent the introduction of gun regulation are also misplaced. Security is best provided by qualified law enforcement supplied using a reasonable budget paid for by taxpayers. A belief in the right to gun possession is misplaced in a developed society and a misinterpretation of the Second Amendment. Without a ready supply of firearms, criminals will find it increasingly difficult and expensive to procure firearms.

The Mythical Black Market

Pro gun advocates claim that there is a black market in guns in Japan, the United Kingdom and Taiwan, all nations with stringent gun restrictions. That may or may not be true, but those countries still have gun death rates orders of magnitude lower than the United States. If that result is the consequence of gun regulation, we urgently need to introduce such measures today. Regulation makes it inordinately difficult for Japanese citizens to procure firearms, and extremely difficult for criminals, which is the intention of gun regulation. Gun restriction works in those countries, and there is no reason it cannot work here.

To say that guns used to commit crimes are either stolen or bought on the black market does not accord with the facts. It is so easy to purchase firearms from gun shows, online or by mail order without a background check that stealing guns or being involved in the black market is just too dangerous. For the average person it is just as easy to buy a firearm legitimately over the counter. It is so absurdly easy that you can even buy a Bushmaster assault rifle while you are grocery shopping at Wal-Mart.

Guns for Everyone

There are few controls on anyone without a criminal record, who can buy any firearm anywhere, other than in certain Northeastern and Pacific states. While there are restrictions on authorized dealers selling to underage youths and felons, that condition vanishes for other types of purchase. People can purchase multiple firearms and ammunition at the same time, without the trade being illegal. The selling of firearms by private sale has almost no restrictions, and the firearm can be sold to almost anyone, including felons, without penalty.

In most states, there are no registration requirements, no paper trails, no restrictions on ammunition, and no restrictions on the type of firearm, with a few small exceptions, no licenses to be purchased, no insurance, and no training requirements. Purchasers are able to buy multiple firearms and unlimited quantities of ammunition at any time, without constraint, and they can sell them to anyone, regardless of identity or prospective usage. Even those with severe mental illness and felons are easily able to obtain firearms, and this is for the most dangerous and deadly implements on Earth today.

Victims Rights

In Minnesota, despite it being a liberal state, legislation preventing gun violence is difficult to pass. When St Paul Democrat, Michael

Paymar opened the hearing of the House Public Safety Committee, he said[13],

> "I recognize that this is a very emotional and complex issue, whenever you're talking about gun control or gun violence. I understand the concerns that some gun owners have about these bills."

A gun is not an emotional issue; it is a collection of metal parts, designed specifically to kill. It is a shame that Rep. Paymar did not mention the concerns that victims of gun violence have about the lack of gun legislation. For those with grave, often life-threatening injuries, gun restrictions are an extremely emotional issue. They should be entitled to an honest, open debate. What is truly emotional and complex is losing a child to senseless gun violence, or a parent, a sibling, a friend or a loved one. There is nothing more complex and emotional that anyone will experience through life. We are so worried about the emotional tribulations of those who wield instruments of great destructive power, and yet we have little sympathy for those who lose loved ones.

I have yet to see the legislators beating their chests about the loss or use of a limb or permanent paralysis caused by gun injury. The concerns of those of us who refuse to bear arms are never at the forefront of the gun debate. It sometimes appears as though we have no rights, feelings, or emotions. We as a society kowtow to the violent, to the destructive, to those who wield death dealing paraphernalia, but not to the peaceful, the non-violent, the victims in society, for that is what we have become, the victims of an extreme gun cult. The conversation is always about the rights of gun owners, never about the rights of society, of security and safety from harm.

There is no debate about the responsibility of gun owners to society, of background checks and limited magazines and regulating ammunition purchases. Seldom is there a discussion of the 30,000 that die each year, because good men do nothing to mitigate those deaths.

The victimization of victims' families by the gun lobby after massacres in schools is appalling. Gun lobby websites vilify and insult families who attempt to get gun regulation enacted in response to these tragedies, yet we hear few denouncing their actions.

Minnesota radio host Bob Davis had this to say after the Newtown massacre,

> "And here's the other thing that drives me crazy, they trot out the victims...I'm sorry that you suffered a tragedy, but you know what? Deal with it and don't force me to lose my liberty, which is a greater tragedy than your loss. I'm sick and tired of seeing those victims trotted out, given rides on Air Force One, hauled into the Senate well, and everyone is just afraid - they're terrified of those victims."

This radio host has lost no liberty, and by making statements like this, he only exacerbates the suffering of the victim's families. They have suffered a true tragedy; if he lost the right to own a firearm, he will still live, and work without injury or threat to life and limb; his family will still come to greet him each morning; he has lost no member of his social circle to senseless gun violence. Just consider the terror of the victims while facing the killer, and the realization that they were about to die. There is no fear that Davis can conjure up that would trump what the children in Newtown endured. He attempts to arrogate victimhood that is not his to take and bemoan his own fear, a feeble narcissistic attempt to gain attention through the tragedy of others.

Davis' co-host Tom Emmer claimed that,

> "families are being used as political pawns to advance a liberal anti-gun agenda. It's probably one of the worst political stunts you could do is to use the victims of the tragedy."

Emmer believes that we should not show the evidence of a massacre, the true victims, and give them a platform to show their loss to the nation, that we should just accept the trite, worn statements from the gun lobby. He expects the victims and their families to suffer silently, unheard, while he trumpets his right to demand more guns, more life-altering injury, and more death. The gun lobby and its proxies are trying to say that they want the evidence to go away, along with the data and vivid imagery that illustrates the consequences of gun extremism.

Non-Gun-Owners Have Rights Too

As peaceful people, we should have the right to demand a society free of guns, or the fear of those who possess guns. People should have the right to walk through their own neighborhoods or communities without the fear of armed vigilantes hunting them down, accosting or assaulting them. People should not have to live with the fear of neighbors armed with semi-automatic assault rifles, or society's apprehension of a young man who has stockpiled dozens of weapons and thousands of rounds of ammunition. The gun lobby, along with Congress and the explicit approval of the Supreme Court increasingly strip that right from people and force them to live with the results of a violent society. This violent society is imposed on us not by criminals, but by those who allow violent people free and easy access to firearms.

I have good reasons for not wanting firearms in the society around me. In South Africa I saw the results of too many guns, of the incessant deaths of innocent people by small arms left over from the guerilla war and guns owned by white South Africans. I want to live in a society in which people do not need guns, in which law enforcement uphold rational and reasonable law, not laws enforced by vigilante neighbors.

Members of a household that have not chosen to have firearms in their home have these weapons imposed on them by gun owners. Their risk of death and injury rises significantly with the introduction of these weapons, as well as the risk of intimidation and oppression, and few fight for their right to safety and security. The wider community, too, is not asked for their permission; instead, they are compelled by Congress and the Supreme Court to accept the heightened risk to life and limb.

The gun lobby claims that gun ownership is a human right, which is odd given the loss of life that results from largely unregulated firearms in society. Indeed, the lack of gun restrictions is the greatest violation of human rights. Sacrificing large numbers of people on the altar of your purported right is not a human right; it is what the human rights movement fights against each day in nations around the world. It is somewhat akin to the National Socialists in Germany justifying the Holocaust by claiming that they were only exercising their right to live in a Germany exclusively for the Aryan people and claim their rightful *lebensraum* (living space).

We as a society should demand that law enforcement be present in our communities to the extent that we need protection from violence or predators armed with firearms. The last thing that the unarmed among us need is an untrained gun owner who may or may not have the firearms training or the legal education to understand the limits of the law and the rights of others. We do not need untrained citizens taking the law into their own hands or imposing their interpretation of the law on unarmed residents.

Society must recognize our right to safety and security from owners of extreme weapons, and from laws permitting the lawful killing of others, such as Stand Your Ground laws. The presence of a Second Amendment does not abrogate society's responsibility to the vulnerable among them, to those who bear no arms.

Anti-gun-violence advocates still need to achieve the vehemence that the gun lobby manages in support of its position. They also need to increase the visibility of their groups, including Mayors against Gun Violence and the Brady Campaign to End Gun Violence. Faint heart does not win the gun wars, any more than it ever won fair lady.

Possession and Responsibility

The gun industry and gun owners need to realize that with rights come responsibilities. As with any right, misuse ought to result in its withdrawal. With the putative right to gun possession comes the responsibility to realize that the privilege cannot be imposed on others, that the right of others to believe that they should be able to live in communities that do not have guns should be respected. Once guns are forced on others, their rights have been usurped for the selfish ends of gun owners. We all have to live in society, and that means respecting the rights of those who do not want guns around their children, in their schools, bars, restaurants, night clubs, railcars or government buildings. Just as we all have the right to use the public highways, none of us has the right to ignore traffic signals, exceed the speed limit, weave in and out of traffic or drive on the sidewalk.

When people bring guns into a public space, those firearms are imposed on others whether it is through the fear of the firearm itself, or because people know that even a simple disagreement might end in death or injury. It creates a paramilitary or vigilante society, with people living under threat, or paranoia of those around them. What once might have ended with law enforcement arresting a thief, pickpocket or other miscreant, now deteriorates into an armed brawl, with a death sentence being leveled for even minor and irrelevant infractions.

While gun owners believe in the right to carry firearms in public, it should not be done, out of courtesy for those who are afraid of them, or do not want them in public. To continue to carry firearms despite the concerns of others is dangerous and demonstrates contempt for society. This is what the gun lobby does when it organizes a show of force after a massacre. Imagine if gun regulation advocates invaded gun shows wearing t-shirts with anti-gun slogans, chanting a gun control message. The First Amendment gives them this right, but it would not be polite. Since gun owners insist on imposing their guns on society, gun control advocates should do the same with their anti-gun message.

Starbuck's recently asked gun owners to leave their firearms at home. The coffee seller found that many patrons and employees were uncomfortable with the practice of some gun owners imposing their firearms on others. Gun owners took the right of customers to the safety and comfort of the coffee shop from them, creating a dangerous and fearful environment. Starbuck's was clearly far too polite, and should insist on a gun-free zone in their outlets. The only reason that they did not insist on banning guns is that it "would potentially require our partners to confront armed customers[14]." Most corporations should be aware that they are not in the business of perpetuating gun ownership; many people just want a quiet, safe place to get away from the world. If they love guns, they can find a gun range or gun shop, of which there are far too many. Perhaps those venues should start offering coffee as one of their products.

Supporting Restrictions

The number of Americans who own guns is decreasing, despite growth in the number of guns in America. Of 314 million Americans, about 60 million own almost 300 million guns. Some people own only one weapon, many people own more than five weapons, and others a great deal more. Reports indicate that some people own more than forty weapons and thousands of rounds of ammunition, far more than any reasonable person needs for personal protection. The only feasible reason for owning arsenals of this size is for armed insurrection, which in most nations is considered an act of treason. Only those people that have a deluded fear of tyrannical government taking their guns have any realistic need to own an arsenal of weapons.

According to a CNN analysis, a steadily decreasing number of Americans own two thirds of the nations guns and as many as one third of the guns on the planet[15], despite constituting only 1% of the world's population. A Pew Research Center survey determined that 37% of households had an adult who owned a gun[16]. A solid majority of gun owners were men, a greater number were white. Together, white men own most firearms, while constituting a minority of the U.S. population[17]. Given the lack of gun registration, these data are difficult to verify, but various surveys appear to verify their accuracy.

Most people in the Northeastern United States support gun restrictions, followed by the West. In the South, half the population opposed restrictions, while nearly half in the Midwest felt similarly[18]. In total, a solid majority of the U.S. population favor stricter regulations according to an ABC/Washington post poll[19].

Three quarters of Americans say that they do not feel safer when more members of their community obtain firearms. By a 5-to-1 margin, people say that they do not feel safer when people in their communities begin to carry guns. Despite a belief that Concealed Carry laws reduce crime, no data support the view that Concealed Carry laws have any demonstrable positive impact on crime rates[20].

Politicians in Washington are cowed before the gun lobby, which represents a very small percentage of the U.S. population. Instead of carrying out sensible gun legislation, as the vast majority of the population demand, politicians appear terrified of the repercussions of introducing gun restriction measures. Many of the gun owners demanding fewer gun restrictions are resident in the swing states, which decide presidential elections, giving an insignificant proportion of the population disproportionate control over the levers of government and over the lives of those lost to gun violence.

The Threat to a Peaceful State

Conservatives are relentless in their efforts to force an increasingly violent ideology on peaceful people. Gun possession imposes a severe cost on society, not merely in financial terms, but in human terms, helping to create the conditions for a disintegration of communities, especially disadvantaged, poorer communities. Those who do not possess guns, nor wish to possess them, have to endure a society in which they are palpably less safe than they would be in countries or states with strict gun limitations.

Throughout history, those with superior arms have imposed tyranny on those without arms, or with inferior arms. This is what the gun lobby is imposing on unarmed communities across the country, and increasingly across the world. Mao Zedong's statement that "political power grows out of the barrel of a gun" can be taken as easily to suggest that gun owners can seize power with their arms as that the government might do so.

Those of us who have no guns are increasingly at the mercy of gun owners who possess progressively more efficient and extreme firearms. Since conservatives are closer to the military-industrial complex than are progressives, it is more likely that the military poses a threat to progressive governments than that progressive government poses a threat to gun owners.

Some people assume that civilians or soldiers armed with handguns contribute to public safety. The United Kingdom shows that this is not necessary for a peaceful society. The local constabulary is mostly unarmed, other than with a nightstick, and violent crime with weapons is extremely low. In Japan, although the police forces are armed, gun violence is almost unheard of, as it is in countries like Spain or Poland. Armed law enforcement contribute only to the increasing incidence of shootings of largely innocent civilians, often resorting to armed intervention when none is needed. Additionally, law enforcement agencies within the United States have become increasingly militarized, demonstrating yet again that the prevalence of firearms does nothing to increase public safety.

All across the world, it is the military apparatus and paramilitary forces that threaten the stability of peaceful people, and all of them use small arms to do so. Guerilla groups victimize non-violent people, while forces armed with assault weapons, semi-automatics and other light armaments, lead insurrections.

Terrorists and criminal gangs may use gun shows to bypass the federal NICS background check system, posing a national security threat. Adam Gadahn, an al-Qaeda associate, openly encouraged individual American Muslims to use gun shows to purchase firearms for use in random attacks[21]. He claimed that America is

> "Awash with easily obtainable firearms. You can go down to a gun show at the local convention center and come away with a fully automatic assault rifle, without a background check..."

The flooding of our towns and cities with millions of unregulated, unregistered firearms and excessive quantities of ammunition is a recipe for disaster. The carnage that could be visited on the American people by this firearm insanity in the event of social breakdown could dwarf human disasters around the world. It is possible that it could be the proximate cause of social breakdown, as has proven to be the case in so many hotspots around the world, from the Congo, to Mozambique and Angola, the Sudan, Ethiopia and Somalia. The American people deserve a more secure, safe environment in which to live, free of the fear of firearm crime and the depravations of gun possession.

In many states, Open Carry advocates insist that it is their right to openly carry and display firearms in public spaces[22]. This is claimed under their liberties, and any regulation is declared a violation of that liberty. By so doing, they are violating the rights of peaceful people who are opposed to having firearms imposed on them and making their environment less secure. Just as people may have the right to Free Speech, that does not give them the right to impose it on people unwilling to listen. These groups are forcing themselves and their beliefs on others, arrogating the rights and liberties of those people, which creates an environment of fear for law-abiding non-gun owners.

Law-abiding, responsible gun owners would accept that others too have rights and would respect their right to live a safe, secure life. That many do not is a clear demonstration of their lack of responsibility and their contempt for the rights of others. It is also disturbing that they defy local ordinances to carry those firearms. The presence of these groups is worryingly reminiscent of paramilitary groups that perpetrate reigns of terror across the globe and throughout history.

Gun Control Loses Elections

The idea that implementing gun controls lose Democrats elections appears somewhat plausible, given the extreme response to gun control measures by the gun lobby. Many Democrats lost their seats in the 1994 mid-term elections. This was attributed to the implementation of the federal Assault Weapons Ban (1994) and Brady Handgun Violence Prevention Act (1993). Weapons bans certainly animate the conservative base, but it is more likely that the standard dynamic in force during midterms is a more powerful motivator. The president's party often loses seats in the midterms. The NRA has had little success in getting its candidates elected in any election. Additionally, Democrats who lost their seats in 1994 were most often in conservative districts.

It is likely that given a choice between the safety and security of their children, and the possession of firearms, the weight of women's vote for children would sway the election.

Society Has Rights Too

One man with a gun can control 100 without one (**Vladimir Lenin**)

The fight for sanity in our gun safety laws is not by any means over. In many ways it's just beginning (**Michael D. Barnes**)

Societies Rights

The residents of any society have a right to expect to be safe in their persons, safe from violence, from theft, from rape, torture, murder and kidnapping. This is why we form societies, a communal effort to benefit from the security of large groups of people. Societies form law enforcement agencies in order to safeguard the community from the violence inherent in lawlessness, and implicit in anarchy. In this society, we have a Constitution, and the purpose of that Constitution is to protect the People from the unwarranted actions and predation of others in that society, whoever they may be, not merely from the iniquities of overreaching government.

The Second Amendment, regardless of the putative claims of the gun lobby, is primarily an attempt to keep the society safe from external threat and internal insurrection. The People also have the right to be safe from those who exploit and misinterpret the Second Amendment to advance a financial or political agenda. We have the right to be free from the fear of death or injury by guns, the right to walk through shopping malls, restaurants, movie theaters and college campuses without fear that someone armed with an assault rifle will start randomly killing people.

Freedom is not the ability to own something, or to place the lives of others in jeopardy, it is the discretion to possess or not possess without fear, to be part of societies activities and structure without trepidation. Just as, with the First Amendment, the People have the right to freedom of religion, so too do they have the right to freedom from religion or religious coercion. If they do not have this right, to be free of religious or other forms of speech coercion, the Amendment, and the Constitution, is of little value other than to oppress or intimidate.

The same can be said of the Second Amendment, that we have the ight to be safe from Second Amendment prostitution. The gun lobby has created a society of fear, suspicion and apprehension, where someone else's freedoms can take our lives from us; if we are not free to live life without anxiety and dread, we are not free. We should be protected by the officials who we have elected and from armed thugs who we did not. The choices made by gun owners can take my life, or the lives of my loved ones; that is not freedom.

If as a society, we demand that our elected officials regulate firearms to assure us that we are safe from violent gun owners, no law, no act of Congress, no Constitution should preclude us from demanding that security. In a Democracy, we choose how to order our society, and if that includes regulating the right to own firearms, that is our right. If we cannot so choose, the Constitution becomes nothing more than the instrument of tyranny, used to impose a violent ideology on an otherwise peaceful society.

Our society is under armed threat, and the gun lobby is preventing us from dealing with those threats by refusing to allow for reasonable gun restrictions. It is as though we were enmeshed in civil war and prevented from halting those attacks by the continued supply of armaments to the belligerents, thus forcing residents to accept those attacks as part of living in society.

Responsibility to Society

It is understandable that people are concerned about gun violence and want to protect their families and friends, neighbors, and others in their social circle. Gun proponents believe that society is under siege and that they need firearms to protect themselves. Paradoxically, by their actions, they are making society far more dangerous, especially for their spouse, children, friends and communities who are exposed to higher levels of risk by exposure to firearms in the home. In addition, they impose a risk on society in exchange for what they perceive, incorrectly, to be dealing with the risks to their own families.

Gun possessors spend much time talking about the rights to their arms, but almost no time at all talking about their responsibilities to society. The extreme gun owner does not appear willing to accept that in a sophisticated society, we all, gun owners included have a responsibility to that society. The pro-gun lobby insists on access to any weapon, anywhere, regardless of the rupture to the fabric of a peaceful society.

The Supreme Court rulings in the *Heller* case that the Second Amendment guarantees a personal right to bear arms and in the *McDonald* case that this guarantee extends to state and local communities in addition to the federal government, imposes deadly force on all the members of a community. These two rulings are being used increasingly by gun extremists to force communities to allow firearms in public places, restaurants, movie theaters, shopping malls and on the streets, stripping the right of communities to decide for themselves what will make them safer.

Society has a right to demand that people act in a responsible way, just as we demand that drivers stay in their lanes, and obey speed limits, road signs and controlled intersections. That so many gun owners made no reasonable demands for restrictions after Newtown demonstrates contempt for socially responsible behavior, a lack of concern at the destruction that their habits have wrought on society, and their lack of empathy for the victims.

The lack of responsible behavior should not be the burden of society to bear; it should be the burden of gun possessors to enforce compliance on their members. If the gun community as a whole is incapable of controlling those around them, they should have the rights to own firearms revoked. Society should not have to bear the reckless behavior of some members of a certain community without recourse to the law. We introduce laws regulating racketeering, drug trafficking and other socially undesirable behavior. We should do the same with firearms. The idea of self-regulation, as proposed by some in the gun community plainly just does not work, and never has. Society needs to change that.

Gun Owners Reaction to Gun Violence

The mother of the Newtown killer Adam Lanza was a "survivalist" who armed herself with firearms she should never have had. Her imprudent behavior towards society enabled her son, whether he was disturbed or not, to take control of her firearms and destroy the lives of children, their teachers and a community. Many in the gun community, instead of being outraged that one of their own had been so negligent in her firearm handling, were outraged that anyone would want to control their ability to procure firearms.

This perverse reaction demonstrates how oblivious to reality certain members of that community can be. Truly responsible, law abiding gun owners should immediately have demanded laws that restricted firearms to irresponsible people, put in place regulations that tested whether people knew enough to properly secure their firearms and reduced access to highly destructive weapons. Gun owners should have insisted on proper training for gun purchasers, and on child locks and other approaches to prevent children from obtaining or using firearms, and condemn those who do not adhere to these rules. Gun sellers should ensure that those to whom they sell are properly trained and licensed, pass background checks, and are no danger to themselves or society.

More gun owners should condemn gun violence in the strongest possible terms whenever and wherever it happens. It is contemptible that some feel that their first reaction should be to demand more guns whenever a violent event occurs. Those owners appear to care little about the lives of vulnerable members of society, especially those that do not feel the need to carry destructive weapons.

Gun owners should adhere to a few basic rules. In the home, firearms should be locked in a safe with a sufficiently secure combination lock or set of keys not accessible to children or other members of the household. If children are present in the home, owners should understand the risks of gun ownership to children. Ammunition should be kept separately from the weapon and the weapon unloaded. Weapons with a universal history of malfunctioning ought to be discarded. Weapons should have safety features such as a trigger or barrel lock, safety catch, biometric deterrents or a trigger that is difficult for children to depress. The weapon should be properly maintained, clean, and empty at all times.

When traveling with a weapon, it should be properly secured in a locked vehicle out of sight and disabled. All members of the household in which weapons are kept should be properly trained in their use. Children should be disallowed from using these weapons, including as gifts. When displaying a weapon openly in public, precautions should be taken to ensure that others cannot take it from the owner. Failure to take these precautions demonstrates a lack of responsibility to society and to the members of a household.

Gun owners who are not responsible in securing their weapons and allow their weapons to be stolen are in essence arming people who may have criminal intent. Equally, those who allow weapons to fall into the hands of children are placing their entire family and community at risk. Many of those involved in criminal acts are armed with stolen weapons, obtained because of gun owners' absence of judgment.

Gun Owners and Gun Restrictions

Gun proponents argue that gun restrictions and control laws are targeting law-abiding citizens, but that is true of all laws. Many people will do the honorable and moral thing ; it is because of those who do not that we introduce laws. If everyone obeyed the laws against murder, we would have no need for those laws, that we do have them is to punish those who refuse to act in a responsible way. People cannot be relied upon to do the right thing; therefore, society has an obligation to protect itself from those people.

Gun advocates insist that they should be able to possess weapons without any safety features. They claim that such things as trigger locks and biometric devices are just a form of gun control. By so doing, they demonstrate apathy towards the safety of those around them, including children and other vulnerable members of their household. If gun advocates refuse to take even the slightest precaution to make firearm ownership safer, society has no reason to trust them with firearms. We as a society insist on safety precautions for people working on construction sites or around dangerous equipment, such as hard hats or safety goggles, leather gloves, and workmen's shoes and no one complains about that, because it makes for a safer work environment. Workmen on construction sites understand the dangers of working around hazardous equipment and they take reasonable precautions; so too should firearm owners.

When I was drafted into the South African Defense Force, we carried automatic rifles, with no ammunition. On the two or three occasions that we went to the firing range, we were issued with the precise number of rounds required for the training. We were told when to fire, for each round we fired. After each round, our NCO's collected the empty shell casings. At the end of the training session, we were required to unload our magazines from the weapon and pull back the breach slide for inspection to show that it was empty. Immediately on return to base, we were required to dismantle, clean and oil the rifle. Only on guard duty were we issued with fully loaded magazines, with a restraining device on the magazine, which had to be broken in order to load the rounds. Other than that, no ammunition was allowed on base outside combat conditions. Any violation of these rules could lead to severe penalties. Civilians in the U.S. are given far more latitude, and it shows conspicuously in the number of civilian deaths we are expected to condone.

Our society should punish people who violate basic rules concerning firearms, including having loaded firearms around children, or unsecured firearms, assault weapons, silencers and other devices that produce more deadly weapons. People who are already responsible in their actions, and have nothing to hide should be unconcerned if common sense laws are introduced that restrict what people may do with their firearms. They should demand that if they are willing to be responsible, others should be compelled to do so. We are not children, but if we act like petulant children, we should be treated as such.

In 1998, a representative national poll was taken to determine how people would react to a program making it more difficult for criminals and delinquents to obtain guns, as well as reduce gun thefts and illegal gun dealers. To reduce gun injuries by 30%, taxes would need to be raised. The question asked was whether people would vote for or against the program. Seventy-six percent reported that they would be willing to pay $50 more in taxes per year, 64% said they would pay $200 more. Households with children under 18 were prepared to pay $108 more per year to reduce gun violence than households without children[23]. All told, households were prepared to pay $24.5Bn to reduce assault related gunshot injuries by 30%. This is what a responsible society looks like, yet Congress in their infinite wisdom, does nothing to mitigate gun violence. People understand that reducing gun violence is a moral imperative, for which they are willing to pay; Congress has not yet achieved that intellectual epiphany.

Conflict Resolution

In any community in which we find ourselves sharing our public spaces with gun extremists, community residents must live with the fear that a simple disagreement or argument will escalate into a shooting match in which the belligerents and innocent civilians are killed or wounded by stray projectiles. It is a disturbing consequence of ubiquitous gun possession that since more citizens are armed, arguments that once were resolved through a shouting match, fistfight or legal action are now resolved using firearms. For those who do not have firearms or the skills to use them, this is a deadly and immature way to solve simple problems. We can no longer go to our local fast food restaurant without sharing that space with armed men who may or may not be law abiding or responsible.

If some gun owners act in socially undesirable ways, raising their voices, become drunk and disorderly, or take over large areas of a restaurant, or other public space, other customers may be reluctant to request that they leave or moderate their behavior. This only increases the stress of living in the community and the mistrust of those around us. We cannot know whether gun owners will use those weapons on us at any point, which forces other patrons from their own enjoyment of those spaces.

Acceptable Risk.

The ALEC[24] resolution on gun rights[25] claims that 99.8% of lawfully owned guns will never be used in a crime. Something similar could be said of motor vehicles; 99.8% of motor vehicles will never have an accident in which someone dies. Every year in the United States, around 33,000 people die because of guns. More than 10,000 are homicides (this figure fell in 2012 to 8,896), with almost 20,000 suicides and the rest a combination of accidental shootings and legal interventions. Katherine Christoffel, MD, writes in the American Journal of Public Health that the U.S. has experienced a transition from an epidemic of firearm injuries in the mid 1980's and early 1990's to endemic firearm injuries and death[26]. As with any endemic condition, society needs to address the ongoing toll of injury and death, just as it does with infectious disease, heart disease or tobacco related illness.

In 2012, the United States had an estimated population of 314 million people[27]. The annual risk of homicide, given 11,101 gun homicides[28], is 1 in 28,285. In 1973, the FDA adopted a figure of one chance in 100 million of a compound increasing the individual risk of developing cancer. By 1977, the acceptable lifetime risk of death from exposure to a carcinogenic compound was amended to 1 in 1 million[29], which for the average individual lifespan of 72 years translates to 1 in 13,888 per year. The risk of dying in any two years from gun homicide thus exceeds the acceptable lifetime risk of dying from a carcinogenic compound. That risk should be unacceptable to agencies such as the Centers for Disease Control and Prevention.

If we include all deaths by gun, the acceptable risk figure is exceeded in less than a year and if we include firearm injuries, that risk is dramatically higher. Guns should thus be categorized as extremely hazardous to health, and properly regulated, as we do with any agent that may cause premature death.

In the late 1980's and early 1990's up to 1993, young people were dying at an unprecedented rate, with the number of firearm deaths peaking at 39,595 in 1993. Various measures were introduced including gun buy backs, dealing with rogue gun dealers, tougher criminal penalties and the collection of data on gun death[30]. Officials understood that they were dealing with exigent circumstances and dealt with the problem accordingly. The net result was falling rates of gun possession and falling death rates. By reducing gun deaths, reasonable gun restrictions did what they were supposed to do.

In 1994, the Assault Weapons Ban passed through Congress, subsequent to the Brady Handgun Violence Prevention Act in 1993. The death rate by firearm fell every single year through 2000 to a low of 28,663[31]. Since the expiration of the Assault Weapons Ban in 2004, firearm deaths have risen from 29,569 to 33,563 in 2012. While the decline may be explained by better policing, higher abortion rates, higher incarceration and the introduction of unleaded petrol, it is unclear why the homicide rate increased subsequent to the expiration of the AWB, other than the greater availability of extreme firearms. What it does show is that common sense gun reforms and regulations do not increase the death rate, and may have a significant influence in causing it to decline.

There is a risk that an outbreak of firearm violence can flare up, infecting other parts of the world. An armed insurrection in this country could easily overflow into surrounding nations. Already, arms trafficking from the U.S. has dramatically increased the flow of illegal guns into Mexico, helping to fuel that countries disastrous drug war. We should not impose our irresponsibly misinterpreted Second Amendment on a nation like Japan, which has the lowest gun death rate on Earth, or on our neighbors, like Mexico.

We regulate pram deaths, or sue manufacturers for wrongful death, when there are only one or two deaths a year, and yet gun manufacturers are allowed -- by law -- to get away with complicity in the death of 30,000 people every year. We do not insist on safety standards for guns, but we insist on seatbelts in cars, helmets for kids on bikes, and traffic lights at intersections. The gun industry is able to sell products shown to kill and injure people without the fear of penalty.

Nowhere else on Earth can one go into a supermarket and shop for a Bushmaster AR-15. Every country determines the acceptable level of risk for each national event: in Switzerland each year a number of people die skiing off a steep mountainside; in Spain, bulls gore a small number of people to death in the ring; in motor sports, a few people die fiery deaths. In the United States, we are forced by the gun lobby to accept the unduly high risk of death by gun in any given year, without any recourse to the courts or the ability to regulate firearms.

We ban cigarettes in public places, or punish drivers for driving drunk, but we allow anyone with sufficient capital and a pulse to buy a gun. In Spain, there is a sensible debate about ending bullfighting. In the United States, we cannot even pass a ban on high capacity magazines or military-style assault weapons.

The gun lobby would have us believe that we should do nothing to mitigate firearm violence, since to do so would in their minds, violate the Second Amendment. There is nothing in the Second Amendment that precludes society from implementing restrictions and prevention. Nor is there any ruling by the Supreme Court that would prevent such restrictions. That Congress will not restrict firearms is an indictment of their lack of concern for the victims of gun violence and their families. Thus, they acknowledge that there is an acceptable risk posed by firearms that society is forced to endure.

Just as in the 1980's under Presidents Reagan and H.W Bush, gun deaths can flare up once more to the levels they were in those years. We need to take drastic action to ensure that society is inoculated against this eventuality. This is why gun regulation is so crucial to the safety and security of families and the nation.

As the worlds leading exporter of firearms, the U.S. finds it reasonable that the profits engendered by the trade in firearms are acceptable even in light of the hundreds of thousands of people who die from firearm violence around the world each year. This mirrors the prevailing conservative attitude that profit is more important to society than human or any life.

Guns to the Left of Them, Guns to the Right

*Apparently, the heart of opposition to new gun regulation is in the white community. Yet, white people face far less daily violence with guns (**Juan Williams**)*

An article by ABC News produced the following statistics; there are 129,817 federally licensed firearm dealers in the U.S.[32]. In comparison, there are 143,839 gas stations[33], 37,053 grocery stores[34], and 14,098[35] McDonalds restaurants. The access to these merchants of death, firearm dealers that is, has grown out of all proportion to the need for personal protection or other uses. When many gun owners have more than a dozen weapons, the liberty extended to them has been taken to extremes. No individual realistically needs an arsenal to protect life and property. Most other developed nations restrict the number and type of weapon any person can own.

In 2010 alone, there were 5,459,240 new firearms produced in the U.S., with at least 95% for domestic consumption[36]. An additional 3,252,404 firearms were imported into the U.S. Each day, 37,500 gun sales, including 17,800 handguns, are completed in the United States[37]. The increase in the number of guns in American society dramatically increases the number of illicit guns that are found on the streets, which may be used to commit violent crimes. In 1994, more than 250,000 households had at least one firearm stolen, with more than 600,000 firearms stolen during these burglaries[38], almost 10% of the total firearms purchased. According to the Justice Department, between 2005 and 2010, 1.4 million firearms were stolen[39]. In 2007, after inspections of only 9.3% of federal firearm licensees across the nation, the ATF reported more than 30,000 firearms missing firearms from dealers' inventories[40].

Buddy, Can You Spare a Gun: The Straw Purchase

Straw purchases, in which a friend, family member or girlfriend buys a firearm for a convicted felon or other prohibited person, is the most frequent method used to divert firearms out of lawful commerce where they are regulated, and onto the street, where they are not[41]. At least half of trafficking investigations carried out by the ATF involved straw purchasers[42].

A study produced by Mayors Against Gun Violence found that gun traffickers used select retail stores from which guns were easy to buy. In one instance, a trafficker returned to the same Pennsylvania store 15 times to purchase 27 firearms within nine months in exchange for crack or cash. In Georgia, traffickers bought 26 guns during seven visits to a single store, reselling the guns on New York streets where restrictions are tighter[43]. One trafficker serving seven years for his crimes bought 55 firearms in five visits to the same store.

The study found that more than 100 guns were purchased by the leader of "*one of the most prolific, profitable and violent drug trafficking organizations*" in the nation, from the same Connecticut dealer[44]. The trafficker served six years in prison, and once released returned to the same store and purchased firearms using straw purchasers, the identical technique used before. The storeowner specifically instructed him on the use of techniques to avoid multiple sale reporting and the attention of law enforcement.

Gang members will often accompany a straw purchaser into a gun store where the owner and employees know the gangs, and buy firearms, often .22 pistols because they are easy to conceal[45]. Money is openly exchanged between the trafficker and the purchaser in front of retail staff, since buyers cannot be trusted with money. Buyers are often high on cocaine or other illicit drugs when making these purchases. They are able to buy the weapons despite this, and are often welcomed by employees as VIP customers. Traffickers will often bargain with dealers before turning the sale over to the straw purchaser.

Store employees in some stores report that straw purchases are a common occurrence. When some employees attempt to prevent the sales, they are overridden by their management, who are clearly aware of the arrangements. Some storeowners even coach prospective purchasers on how to get others to buy firearms in their stead.

These buyers often know nothing at all about the firearms that they are purchasing, according to this study, and gun dealers recognize this, but do nothing to stop the trade. Traffickers may also use coercion to get straw purchasers to buy weapons, including threats of violence against buyers or their families.

Many stores will reject a sale if they recognize an attempted straw purchase, but many gunshop employees have no training whatsoever in spotting these purchases. Many employees have no idea what a straw purchase is, and sell to anyone who checks the required federal forms correctly.

Straw purchasers know that the weapons might be traced back to them, especially if those weapons are trafficked to others who then commit crimes. The purchasers are most often not traffickers themselves; rather they are pawns of the traffickers, and an unwitting part of a criminal conspiracy, rather as drug mules become pawns of the drug cartels.

Reducing the flow of weapons trafficked to the secondary market may effectively raise the street price of those weapons, allowing fewer felons to obtain firearms by this method. Since high-risk groups who may live in poverty use many illicit weapons, any price rise is an obstacle in the acquisition of firearms.

The Gun Show Loophole

Most Americans believe that with freedom comes responsibility -- and that one measure of responsible gun ownership is a background check. There must be an app for that. **(Christine Pelosi)**

The term "gun show loophole" is somewhat of a misnomer, since private sales of all types are exempt from NICS background checks. The loophole allows around 40% of guns traded to slip through the federally mandated background check system. For those purchases made with criminal intent, this is around 80%. These shows provide an ideal avenue for prohibited persons, traffickers, gangs, felons, terrorists and others to obtain firearms without the dangers of purchasing illicit firearms on the streets. Some claim that these shows are part of the American local tradition of free trade within the secondary firearm market. Historically, trade has been and is restricted on any number of dangerous goods, including illicit drugs, pharmaceuticals, alcohol and cigarettes. There is no reason that extreme weapons should not be similarly regulated.

The very lack of background checks and other traceable data make it exceedingly difficult for law enforcement to determine the extent of criminal activity at gun shows. Much information is anecdotal, or based on the retrieval of guns after the commission of a crime.

In April 2000, President Clinton spoke to Tom Brokaw in a Town hall meeting in Denver[46]. They were speaking about the recent massacre at the school in Columbine, and gun regulations. Clinton indicated that he supported closing the gun show loophole, especially after the killings at the school. Thirteen years later, the gun show loophole still exists; Congress refuses to close it despite the evidence that it allows people otherwise not authorized to buy guns, to purchase personal weapons. The President emphasized the need for child safety locks, safe gun technology and large ammunition clips. To date, nothing has been done, primarily because of the political intimidation of the gun lobby.

The President mentioned waiting periods of 72 hours, but even the 24-hour waiting period was too long for the gun lobby, which believes that there is a compelling need to own a gun immediately. The gun lobby opposes background checks despite the fact that it only takes a few minutes. The only reason that a background check might take longer is if there is something of concern in the check, which is precisely the point. Society has a right to ensure that guns do not fall into the wrong hands. According to President Clinton, over 90% of checks can be completed in 24 hours. It is difficult to believe that an adult, who has waited twenty years to possess a firearm, suddenly feels a compelling need to own one in seconds. If he has nothing to hide, a few weeks wait should not be problematic.

The President said that after the signing of the Brady Bill, which used background checks, "a half million people who were felons, fugitives and stalkers haven't gotten their handguns." He continued, *"Gun crime is down 35% since I took office and we have the lowest homicide rate in 31 years."*

The single reason for gun lobby opposition to changing the gun show loophole is that when customers leave, it gives them a chance to think about their purchase and they may decide not to buy. The gun lobby is in the business of selling guns for the gun manufacturers and any such background check would impede that business.

There is a simple way around that, as suggested by President Clinton, and that is to hold the gun in escrow until the background check has been completed, then deliver the gun to the new owner. The weapon can be paid for, and ready to deliver once the background check is completed. That way, the sale is completed, which helps the business, and a reasonable waiting period is mandated, which satisfies gun restriction advocates.

The Gun Show is the ideal way for criminals or those of violent intent to obtain a firearm without any check whatsoever. There is no way to tell whether a person coming in to a gun show is responsible or not, whether they are criminal or not, or whether they have violent intentions or Severe Mental Illness. More guns end up on the street in criminal gangs because of the gun show loophole, and more young people die as a result.

It is not so much that the gun show loophole is at fault for allowing prohibited persons from obtaining firearms, it is also the transfer between private parties or family members that allows so many illegal guns on to the street.

Crime Guns and Gun Shows

A 1999 review of ATF data shows that substantial numbers of guns originating from gun shows were being used in drug crimes and violent crimes, as well as passed illegally to minors[47]. Many sellers openly advertise that background checks are not needed, and that only age and an address are required for purchase. The review also indicated that the shows "*provide a ready supply of firearms to prohibited persons, gangs, violent criminals and illegal firearms traffickers*". A 2000 report found that at least 14% of ATF investigations of illegal trafficking involved gun shows and flea markets, or around 26,000 illegally diverted firearms[48].

Federal Firearm Licensees have informed the ATF that prohibited people are acquiring firearms at these shows without a background check. ATF investigations show conclusively that gun shows are centers of criminal activity. At least 46% of ATF gun show investigations involve felons trading firearms. According to the review, investigations showed that more than a third of the firearms involved were used in subsequent crimes[49]. Anecdotal evidence suggests that the majority of illicit activity at gun shows is never investigated by the ATF. During the 2004-2006 period, the ATF only initiated 202 investigations at 195 gun shows, yielding 121 arrests and 5,345 firearms seized[50]. More than 6,000 gun shows were held during that period. It is unrealistic to believe that straw purchases and other illicit activities were not happening at those shows.

An undercover operation by New York City into seven gun shows in Nevada, Ohio and Tennessee produced some interesting findings. Sixty-Three percent of private sellers indicated that they would sell to a purchaser who would not pass a background check. Ninety-four percent of licensed dealers were prepared to sell to apparent straw purchasers. Additionally, many sellers were "*engaged in the business of selling firearms without a license*"[51]. Some unscrupulous licensed dealers also use these shows to hide off the book sales. This allows even a small number of dealers to feasibly transfer large numbers of guns into the illicit market[52].

A report by the Americans for Gun Safety Foundation conducted on gun shows concludes that criminals easily access firearms at gun shows. According to the same report, any law requiring background checks would not place obstacles in the way of routine gun show business[53]. The report shows that states that do not mandate gun show background checks are inundating the nation with crime guns, with most out-of-state crime-guns originating in states without gun show background checks.

It is hardly surprising that many gun owners see background checks as an ineffective tool preventing prohibited persons from obtaining firearms. With the gaping loophole in firearm laws, almost anyone can obtain a firearm on the open market. The gun lobby openly encourages and promotes the absence of laws that might prevent felons and others from obtaining firearms at gun shows.

New Jersey is a state with relatively low gun deaths and injuries and stricter gun controls than other states. Gun shows are particularly rare in the Garden State, with only one regularly held event, in which antique guns are traded, demonstrating the benefits of stricter laws. In contrast, Texas, a state with sharply higher death and injury rates, holds more than 150 events each year[54].

Private Transfers, Gun Shows and Gun Trafficking

Many transfers between buyers and sellers are private, undocumented and involve no background checks. Only California has made such transfers illegal, which reduces deaths and injuries, as well as improving the ability of law enforcement to solve crime and track criminal networks[55]. Additionally, law enforcement in the state maintains a presence at gun shows, and designs regulations to cover these events.

In one spot for 20/20 on ABC News, a young man was given $5000 to buy weapons at a gun show to determine how quickly he could spend this sum and how many firearms he could buy. He bought a Glock handgun, with no background check and no questions asked. He proceeded to purchase an AR-15 semi-automatic, three rifles, four shotguns and one handgun over the course of one hour[56]. At one point, he was asked for identification, but the seller relented when he said he did not have any with him. It would have been just as easy for him to resell the firearms in the parking lot. There were no restrictions to whom he might sell, no limit on the number of firearms, or the quantity of ammunition he might purchase.

Even when sellers know a buyer personally, there may still be reasons that the buyer should be barred from owning firearms. Since sellers do not know many of the buyers, there is no way to verify that the buyer is likely to be responsible. As it is, as a society, we do not know whether those who buy firearms are trustworthy, that they are in fact "good guys", especially not without some form of verification.

Felons, Misdemeanants and Crime Guns

Studies show that high-risk individuals pose a significant risk to public safety. Stricter prohibitions on prior prison inmates would reduce gun crimes. A recent study of inmates showed that of those felons who committed their crimes with a firearm, only 27% were prohibited from owning firearms due to a felony conviction. Of these offenders, 60% could legally possess firearms, while the rest were convicted of misdemeanors involving firearms, convicted in juvenile court, or had prior arrests with no convictions[57]. Handgun purchasers with misdemeanor convictions who are legally able to purchase firearms commit violent crimes at a rate two to ten times higher than do handgun buyers with no previous convictions[58]. Those with two or more prior convictions were 15.1 times more likely to be charged with serious crimes. Those denied purchase rights were 25% less likely to be arrested for crimes involving firearms. Purchasers with a history of arrest but no convictions commit crimes at as high or a higher rate than misdemeanants do.

The list of prohibitions should be expanded to include those convicted of drug possession within five years, or those shown to have drugs in their system within two years of receiving a drug test. People with a history of alcoholism, including those with DUI convictions or arrests should similarly be prohibited. Since it has been found that people with Serious Mental Illness who are also using drugs are more likely to commit crimes or suicide, people treated for SMI should be regularly tested for drug use for a reasonable period before being allowed to purchase firearms.

Most violent crimes with firearms are committed by people between the ages of 18 and 25. People within that range ought to be subject to more restrictive gun laws than people over 25. In Israel, people who have not completed military service must be over 27 to purchase a firearm, or over 21 if military service has been completed. Considering that twenty-one is the legal limit for the consumption of alcohol, similar restrictions ought to apply to firearms. Restricting alcohol has led partially to significant reductions in motor-vehicle deaths over the last three or four decades. In contrast, forty-five states allow 18-20 year olds to legally possess as many firearms as they desire[59].

We need to do a better job of keeping firearms out of the hands of people who may pose an elevated threat to society. Society has a right to a modicum of security, despite the unwarranted belief in threats to liberty. There are more important liberties than the putative right to bear arms. Any history of criminal activity, violence, domestic abuse or Serious Mental Illness ought to be seen as factors keeping people from possessing firearms. Society should expect that only those shown to be responsible should have the privilege to own firearms.

With the freedom of access allowed by the Internet, online gun sales are rising strongly. Given the inadequacy of background checks, almost anyone can order almost any weapon online. People who otherwise would require a background check, such as felons, the seriously mentally ill, youths, domestic violence abusers, and those with terrorist or gang affiliations can buy firearms without any verification whatsoever. No identification is needed to buy weapons or ammunition online. With such a largely unregulated market, there is little reason for people to buy firearms from gun retailers and undergo a background check. This provides an open gateway for massive sales to criminal organizations, terrorists, and other undesirable individuals.

An investigation by the office of New York Mayor Michael Bloomberg found that[60],

> "There is a vast and largely unregulated market for illegal weapons, with 62 percent of private sellers willing to provide firearms to people who were not likely to pass a background check".

After the massacre in Newtown, some selling organizations, such as TV station KSL in Salt Lake City, temporarily suspended online classifieds firearms listings[61]. The question is, if they saw that selling firearms online could pose a moral dilemma for society and for the station, why they did not shut it down permanently. A moral imperative is not temporary, just to satisfy viewers or the guilty conscience of the management of the station. If there was a problem after Newtown, that problem still exists. Responsible websites like

EBay, Craigslist, Amazon and Google prohibit the listing of firearms for sale[62].

Unregulated Ammunition Purchases by Criminals

The NICS system is used to prevent prohibited persons from purchasing firearms, but ammunition is freely available to those people without a background check. A study targeting individuals buying ammunition in Los Angeles in April and May 2004 determined that 2.6% of ammunition purchasers were prohibited from possessing ammunition, including those with previous felony convictions. These felons purchased 10,050 rounds of ammunition during this period[63]. The report concludes that monitoring of ammunition purchases may reduce the supply of ammunition to felons as well as the incidence of injury during gun assaults.

Without ammunition, a firearm is no better than many other objects at inflicting harm on others. Restricting access to ammunition may be a more effective form of gun control than restricting the weapons themselves[64]. City ordinances enacted in Los Angeles, San Francisco, Oakland and other Californian cities requiring tough identification standards for ammunition purchases are thought to be effective in preventing criminals from purchasing ammunition. Research in Chicago finds that such laws make it more difficult for criminals to acquire ammunition than firearms. An alternative would be to produce less lethal ammunition for defensive purposes. The purpose should not be to kill, rather, where possible, to neutralize a compelling threat to life. To insist on the ability to take life is a clear indication of moral depravity.

The Human Cost of Gun Ownership

There will be no justice as long as man will stand with a knife or with a gun and destroy those who are weaker than he is. **(Isaac Bashevis Singer)**

U.S. Death Toll

Every year, more than 30,000 Americans lose their lives to guns. It takes just 36 days for the number of deaths by firearms to exceed the numbers killed in the attacks of 9/11. During the first decade of this millennium, 303,937 people died by gun, which translates to 102 attacks of the magnitude of 9/11. In just two years, the number of deaths for a decade jumped to 309,538, or the equivalent of 104 9/11 attacks. Every day one gun death is a child under 14, while 16 to 18 of the dead are between 15 and 24[65]. Each day 106 people die by firearm, a steady and relentless drumbeat of death and injury.

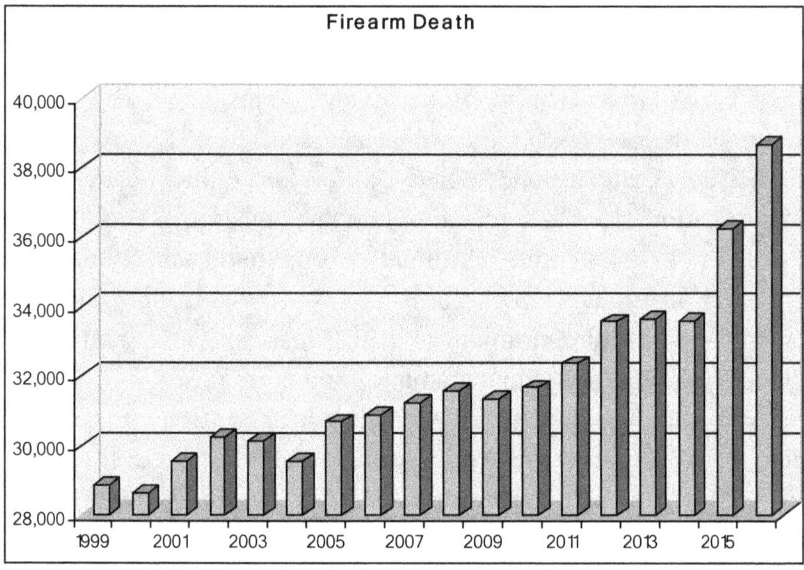

Figure 1 US Gun Deaths 1999 to 2016[66]

It is likely that the high mortality rate contributes to a reduction in American lifespan as compared to other developed nations. The U.S. ranked 30th among men in the 35 most affluent nations. One study found that American men lose 104 days of life due to firearm violence, days not lost in other industrial nations[67]. For African-American men, 297 days of life are lost to firearm homicides.

It takes just three to five years for the number of gun deaths in the United States to exceed the number of people killed by the atomic bomb dropped on Hiroshima, and two to three years to exceed those killed in the nuclear attack on Nagasaki.

It was safer to be an Iraqi civilian during the past ten years of the Iraq war than it was to be a civilian in the United States. Estimates range between 115,000 and 150,000 Iraqi civilians dead, and an additional 24,000 to 37,000 combatant fatalities. In the United States between 2003 and 2011, 279,294 people died by firearm. A greater number of civilians were killed in the United States, a nation with no acknowledged internal war, than in Iraq, a country at war, by a factor of about 2:1. The slaughter in the U.S. by that measure is worse than one of the most devastating wars on Earth in the same period.

Between 1979 and 2011, 1,083,970 Americans died by firearm[68]. This exceeds the total number of combat deaths in all the wars fought by this country since 1776 (848,163)[69], in a mere 32 years. That death toll is twice the number of people killed in the Rwandan genocides (estimates range between 500,000 and 1 million people)[70]. It is also twice the number killed in the Spanish civil war that ushered in the fascist dictatorship of General Francisco Franco; estimates currently put the death toll at ~500,000[71].

Between the years 1933 and 1997, (591,528) Americans were the victims of gun homicide. In the same 64-year period, 1,417,902 Americans were the fatal victims of gun homicide, suicide, unintentional shootings and unknown causes combined[72]. If the years 1999 to 2011 are included, this figure rises to 1,814,736 fatalities. This exceeds the estimates of the number executed by the Khmer Rouge in Cambodia (1.3 million)[73]. It is almost a third of the number of Jewish people killed by the National Socialists in the Holocaust, and about a sixth of the estimated total number of people massacred in the Holocaust[74]. It exceeds the number of Jewish children killed in the Holocaust, who numbered about 1 million. It is also more than the number of people who died in the concentration camp at Auschwitz-Birkenau.

The number of gun injuries sustained by Americans between 1933 and 2011 amounts to an estimated 4,476,129 people, vastly exceeding the total number of wounded in every American war since 1776[75]. It is also almost double the total number of Americans killed and wounded in those wars.

Sarah Brady, wife of the former White House Press Secretary James Brady, a prominent proponent of gun restrictions had this to say,

> "Many Americans face more danger in the streets of their community than our now volunteer armed forces face on an average day. Events in just the last two years demonstrate that schoolchildren, online brokers, Zerox repair workers and even small toddlers at day care centers can face the same threat our soldiers are trained to defeat."

It takes a mere decade for the death toll by gun to exceed the number of Americans killed in combat in the Second World War (291,557), less than two years to exceed those killed in combat in the First World War (53,402), and one and a half years to exceed those killed in combat in Vietnam (47,424)[76].

In Louisiana, the state with the highest rate of firearm death in the nation, between 2001 and 2010, there were 4,519 gun homicides, more than the 4,488 Americans killed by all causes in the Iraq war and more than double the 2,229 killed in Afghanistan[77]. By that token, it would have been safer for the population of Louisiana to move to Iraq or Afghanistan during those years. Mississippi had a similarly elevated death rate, with 2,098 people killed by guns in the last ten years, close to the number of Americans killed in combat in Afghanistan during the same period[78].

Firearm injury is the second leading cause of injury death after motor vehicle crashes. There are an average of five nonfatal firearm injuries for every two firearm deaths. Firearms are involved in 67% of homicides, 50% of suicides, 43% of robberies and 21% of aggravated assaults. Guns account for 6.6% of premature death in this country each year[79].

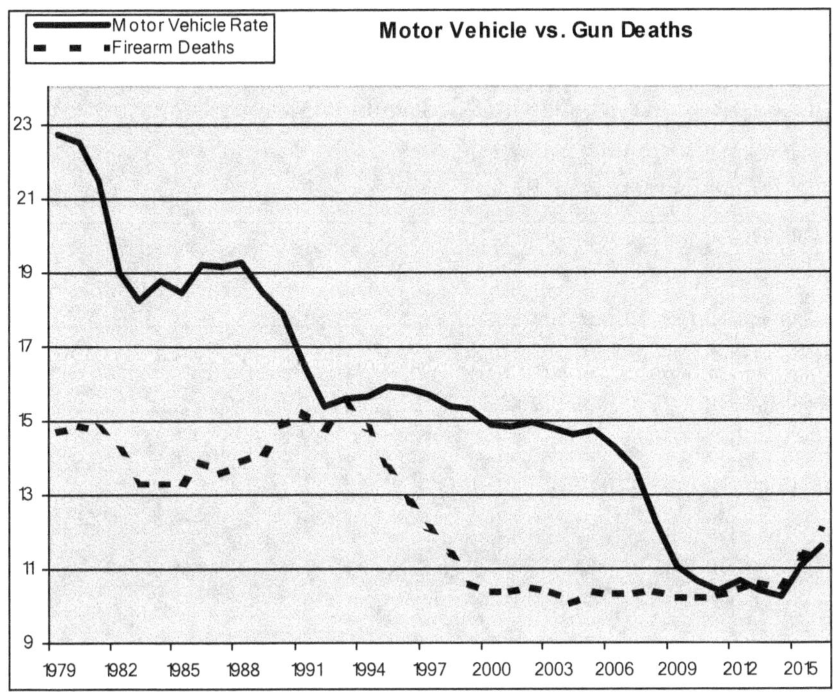

Figure 2 Motor Vehicle vs. Gun Deaths 1979 - 2011

The number of gun deaths between 1979 and 1997 remained relatively constant at 32,689 in 1979 and 32,166 in 1997. The firearm death rate has dropped due to the growing population size, from 14.64 in 1981 to 11.09 in 1998, a relatively small reduction compared to other developed countries. The number of firearm deaths between 1999 and 2010 rose from 28,874 to 31,672, while the rate barely changed from 10.3 to 10.07[80]. Despite this, the gun lobby claims that deaths by firearm have dropped over the last ten years.

The number of deaths by firearm dropped dramatically during Clinton's presidency, from 37,776 to 28,874. During President George W. Bush's term, the number rose to 31,593. This change is feasibly due in part to the implementation of the assault weapons ban in 1994 and its expiration in 2004 and the refusal of the Bush Administration to take action to reduce firearm deaths[81].

The number of injuries resulting from firearms rose significantly between the years 2001 and 2013. In 2001, there were 63,012 injuries caused by firearms compared to 84,258 in 2013, a 33% increase over the twelve years[82]. In the last year of GW Bush's presidency, 2008, injuries peaked at 78,662. In 2013, nonfatal gunshot injuries reached a record with the rate increasing from 22 to 26.6. In twelve years, the injury rate has increased 20%.

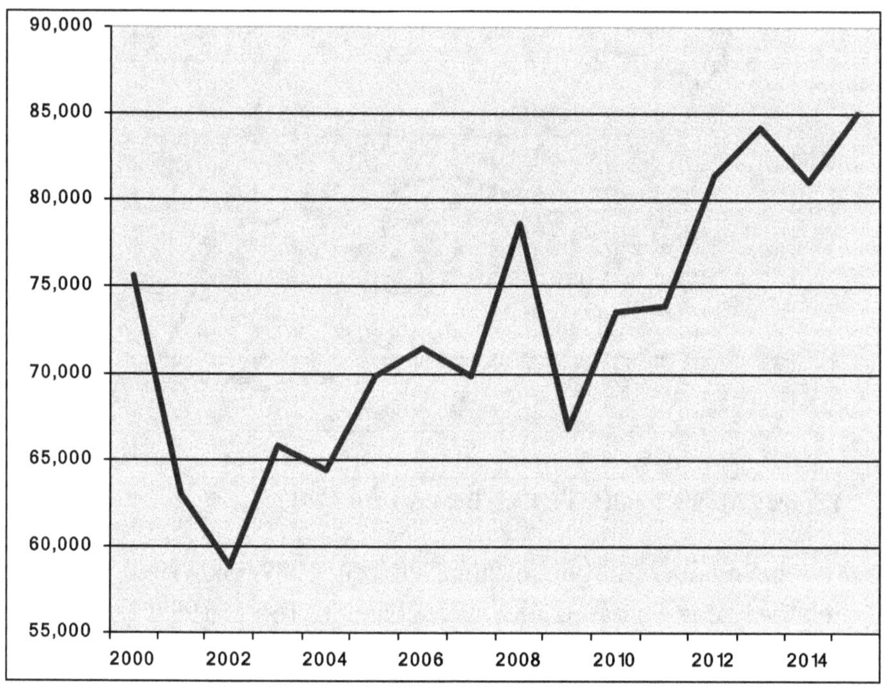

Figure 3 Firearm Injuries 2000 to 2016[83]

The total fatal and non-fatal injuries by firearm between 2001 and 2012, rose from 92,585 in 2001 to 121,249 in 2015[84], a 30% increase over the period. Far from the claims by the gun lobby that gun violence is falling, the figures show a statistically significant rise in gun violence. Considering that trauma surgeons are becoming more successful at treating gunshot victims, the death rate could be much higher in the absence of trained medical staff. In light of that, the figures in the United States compare unfavorably with many developing nations.

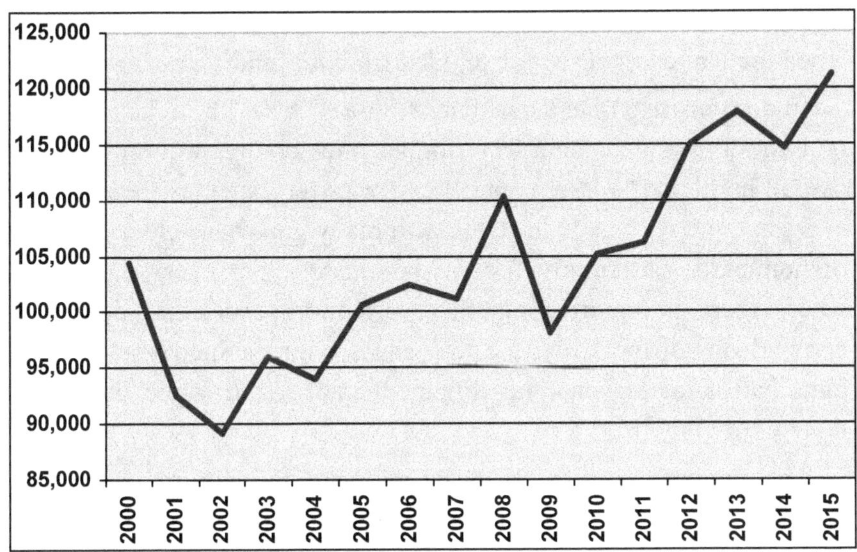

Figure 4 Total Firearm Death and Injury[85]

In the five years preceding the 1994 Federal Assault Weapons Ban, the number of gun homicides ranged between 16,218 and 17,527. In subsequent years, the homicide numbers fell to 15,551 (1995), 14,037 (1996), 13,252 (1997) and 11,798 (1998) [86]. Whether the fall was due to the ban is debatable, but the nation did not see a dramatic increase in deaths or crime during that period. The opposite is the case, demonstrating if not success, the absence of failure of gun regulation legislation.

In the years subsequent to the expiration of the Federal Assault Weapons ban in 2004, the total number of gun deaths rose in almost every year from 2004 (29,569) to 2015 (36,252). Gun homicides during the same period rose from 2004 (11,624) to 2008 (12,179). By 2015, the homicide number had risen to 14,415. The gun homicide rate remained stable between 1998 and 2011.

A study by the CDC in 1998 determined that in 1994 the United States accounted for 45% of gun deaths among the world's 36 wealthiest nations, a rate of 14.24 per 100,000[87]. Studies find that of the homicides in 26 countries, the higher the number of guns available, the more homicides reported[88]. These figures held even when the United States was excluded from the study.

In a comparison between states, those states with higher levels of household gun ownership have higher rates of firearm homicide and overall homicide[89]. After controlling for poverty and urbanization, for every age group, people in states with many guns have elevated levels of homicide, particularly firearm homicide[90]. For every age group, where there are more guns there are more accidental deaths. In comparisons of mortality, the four states with the highest number of guns had a rate seven times higher than the states with the lowest number of guns.[91].

The number of deaths, the death rate and the injury rate by firearm continues to increase, while deaths by all other causes continues to fall. While the firearm homicide rate is relatively stable over the last 15 years, total firearm injuries are up sharply. The age adjusted death rate by all causes declined to a record low in 2008, which includes heart disease and cancer. Only firearm deaths continue to increase, led by firearm suicides[92]. While our nation has successfully addressed every form of violent death, it has done nothing to change the firearm death rate.

Benefits and Detriments of Gun Ownership

Gun proponents argue that there are benefits to firearm possession without specifying with suitably derived empirical evidence what those benefits might be. There was no benefit to the more then 30,000 people who die each year, or the more than 80,000 who are injured badly enough to have to visit an emergency room. In comparison to countries with low rates of firearm fatality, there was no benefit. No benefit was derived for the millions of animals slaughtered each year in pursuit of "sport". In some countries, even law enforcement officers do not use the weapons they carry because there is no gun crime.

Even the belief that you will feel safer if you own a firearm does not withstand scrutiny. Those who are armed are more likely to believe that others are armed, whether this is true or not. They are also more likely to use their weapons to prevent threats that do not exist or against mild threats that ordinarily would not warrant action.

Viewing firearms as a symbol of liberty or democracy is similarly untrue. Those nations with the highest numbers of gun deaths are almost invariably states with few democratic rights, states with high civil unrest and those without functioning central government. None of those facts is true about the United States, a nation in which we invest in law enforcement to protect citizens from harm.

The costs to society are vastly greater than any putative benefits claimed by gun proponents. In consideration of the cost vs. benefits, we should seriously consider a universal ban on all firearms.

The Minimal Cost of Gun Restrictions

Gun proponents also argue that society is unwilling to pay the cost of gun restrictions. We must compare the costs of controlling firearms against the costs of dealing with gun violence. We have a good idea of the costs of gun violence in lives shattered and lost, spiraling medical costs and lost productivity. Societies without significant gun violence do not incur these costs, and firearm restriction comes at a fraction of the cost of gun violence. An analysis in 2002 found that reductions in overall violence in society has led to a return of people to central cities, a change that is worth billions of dollars, as indicated by rising property values[93].

I have found no verifiable studies that show a significant cost to society of gun control when compared to the staggering and rising cost of gun violence. There may be some residual cost of increasing the presence of law enforcement, especially foot patrols, but that only has the effect of reducing all forms of crime, ultimately benefiting society.

The Oppressive Cost to Society of Possessing Deadly Weapons

Gunshot injury and death impose a heavy cost on taxpayers across the country. These costs should be paid for by surtaxes on firearms and ammunition, and by mandated firearm insurance. It is unfair to society to expect that taxpayers pick up the tab for these deaths and injuries, nor is it fair that uninsured victims be forced to pay their own medical costs. It should be incumbent upon those who possess firearms to pay the medical costs of victims and their families, rather than placing the burden on those families. If people are going to insist on firearm ownership, they should be responsible for the death and injuries that result. Road users pay for fatalities and injuries through federally mandated insurance premiums; the same should apply to those who possess firearms. The U.S. taxpayers have to shoulder a financial burden out of all proportion to other nations, just to support an anachronistic and generally misinterpreted Second Amendment.

The costs of gunshot injury to society are not purely medical and productivity losses. The change in life quality and community impact is ultimately far greater. One study by Philip Cook in 1994 determined that the lifetime cost of gunshot injury was around $17,000, an annual $2.3 Billion in medical costs[94].

In 2005, an estimate put the cost of hospital charges for firearm injuries in Pennsylvania at $127 million per year. The median charge for in-hospital care per gunshot injury was $30,814, almost double the figure for the 1996-1998 period. At least 70% of patients with these injuries were either uninsured, or medical assistance patients[95].

U.S. taxpayers pay half the total lifetime costs of treating injuries, with private insurance, victims and others covering the rest[96]. Homicides resulting from firearm injuries can cost taxpayers $244,000 in incarceration costs. In California, the estimated annual cost of incarceration was $47,102 per year, including healthcare, operations, inmate support and rehabilitation[97]. In New York City, the city paid $167,731 per inmate each year by 2013[98]. Taxpayers also cover some costs of the injured, many of which are uninsured, including daily care, medical treatment and rehabilitation. Many victims become eligible for government-assisted housing, disability benefits and education grants, which adds additional burdens to taxpayers[99].

A study in 2008 put the cost of gun violence to federal, state and local government of providing medical care, mental health, emergency transport, policing, criminal justice and lost taxes at $4.7Bn[100] [101]. The cost of firearm fatalities is higher than any other injury related death at around $33,000, while injuries related to firearms exceed $300,000. One study put the total social cost of a single crime-related gunshot wound at $1 million[102]. In Chicago, the decade-long cost of gun related injury is about $2.5 Billion, or $2,500 per household. The homicide rate in Chicago was about 15.9 per 100,000. In Baltimore, it was 31.3 and in New Orleans 57.6[103]. The citizens of those cities were paying increased taxes and intangible costs because of gun violence.

A recent study concluded that gun violence costs American taxpayers at least $12Bn each year in court costs, insurance and hospitalizations paid by governmental health programs. According to this study, society incurs $32 per firearm in death and injury costs annually. The study also calculated that the costs per injury, which include medical and psychiatric care, court cases, insurance and emergency transport, rose from $14,500 in 1992 to $28,700 in 2010[104]. The study found that while drunken driving costs were higher in 1992, the costs of gun injuries now exceed those of drunk driving.

The total direct and indirect annual costs of gun violence to the economy are anywhere between $30Bn and $115Bn depending on the study. Compare that to Canada, where the costs are estimated to be around C$5.1Bn[105]. Clearly, the staggering costs imposed on society by the unwarranted enforcement of putative Second Amendment rights cannot be borne by any society, particularly one with allegedly insurmountable budget deficits. There is no reason that society should have to pay for the deadly possessions of others within that society.

The Financial Burden of Arming Society

After the Newtown shootings, the NRA declared that all schools should have armed guards, which would dramatically raise the direct cost of gun violence to the community and to taxpayers. The addition of metal detectors in schools similarly raises direct costs as well as intangible costs such as anxiety and fear. Metal detectors also infringe on academic freedom, freedom of movement and other basic societal rights.

A society in which armed guards are present in schools and other places, along with metal detectors creates the impression of a society under siege, or a police state, which is something that gun proponents so adamantly oppose. It is ironic that the very solutions proposed by gun proponents themselves result in authoritarianism, or a civilian police state, in which some civilians are armed, representing an implicit threat to those who are not. Additionally, the screening of students would result in significant losses to education time, at a time when budgets are significantly constrained, class time is being cut, and teachers' contracts terminated.

When society allows tens of millions of people to own firearms, it raises the level of risk for society as a whole, but especially for those who feel compelled to buy firearms to protect themselves. As the number of firearms rises in society, deaths and injuries rise, creating a feedback loop in which gun owners believe that they need more firearms and ammunition, or more deadly weapons to protect themselves. They would otherwise not have incurred that cost. The insistence of gun owners on owning firearms for protection costs them in the long term, along with imposing other miscellaneous increased costs on society.

With reductions in gun ownership, society would no longer have to squander scarce sums to insulate itself from gun violence. There would be no need for society to cater to this violence using armed guards at schools, or metal detectors in office buildings and airports, emergency response units, trauma centers, and law enforcement, all of which could be used for other pressing exigencies. The budgetary increases required for protection and prevention by allowing gun possession could be used for something more productive. Actively working to reduce gun violence would lead to lower preventive costs, a revival of blighted inner city neighborhoods and increased economic prospects for residents.

The Intangible Burdens on the Injured

Injured victims of gun violence experience productivity losses, chronic medical costs, disability, ailments affecting their physical abilities and psychological trauma. Victims can end up with debilitating injuries, paralysis and traumatic brain injury. A 2000 book by Philip Cook, et al, highlighted the real ongoing costs of gun violence including the time spent waiting at metal detectors in buildings and airports, reductions in property values due to gun crime and other intangibles. When all these factors and others are considered, this research estimates the cost to the nation at as much as $100Bn annually[106].

The gun lobby claims that gun ownership is about saving or preserving life, and yet self-defense uses by gun are relatively low. The $100Bn in gun death and injury costs to society could easily be used to provide health care to millions of Americans, saving vastly more lives than are claimed for self defense by firearm. If the gun industry were truly concerned about saving life, they would lobby for fewer firearms and more health care.

The Small Arms Survey produced a report that assesses the costs of small arms violence that highlights the problem. Indirect tangible costs of firearm injury to the injured party and to the community include productivity losses, social capital investment losses, life insurance cost, and indirect protection. Costs to the economy include production loss, property value, tourist streams and foreign direct investment. Intangible costs to the victim encompass quality of life, including pain and suffering, reduced job opportunities, access to schools, public services and participation in community life[107].

None of these costs to the injured is recovered from the gun owner, the gun community or the arms industry, despite the increased risks imposed on society by those groups. The burden is placed on the injured party.

The Intangible Burdens on the community

The death of a member of a community means the loss of his contribution to that community, to his family who may rely on his income, or a future income in the case of youths. In communities blighted by gun violence, controlling that source of death and injury can produce more stable communities, and productive residents, which creates benefits beyond the community.

The cost of life insurance premiums for all Americans may be higher in part because of the higher risk of death by firearm. Some estimates put this increased cost at $2Bn annually. Guns account for a significant reduction in life expectancy in the U.S. compared to other causes of death. Firearm prevalence reduces the life expectancy of U.S. residents by 104 days, in comparison to lung cancer, which reduces life expectancy by 197 days. The impact of firearms on life expectancy may account for at least 27% of the reduced life expectancy of U.S. male residents compared to other developed nations[108].

Communities across the U.S. that experience excess gun violence may change their behavior as they adapt to the threat and fear of firearm violence. Families may have to care for victims of this violence with limited resources, such as medical insurance, as well as the continuing fear of endemic violence in their communities. This in turn, particularly for victims and their families, may cause Post Traumatic Stress, with its associated complications, depression, aggression and anxiety[109]. The continuing threat posed to families may also lead to illegal concealed carry as people feel the need to protect their families. This ultimately creates a cycle of violence, and the formation of gangs that foment greater unrest, and serious injury and death by firearm.

Increased levels of crime in inner cities due to gun violence leads residents and businesses to move to safer neighborhoods in the suburbs, which increases traffic flows and congestion. Residents who have no choice but to remain in blighted areas are often unable to leave their homes for fear of gunfire. Law enforcement may refuse to enter certain neighborhoods, particularly with assault-style weapons freely available. Schools may deteriorate, leading to a dirth of opportunity for poorly educated children, and increased levels of crime, alcoholism and lawlessness.

The perception of gun violence will preclude tourists from visiting cities, or restricting their visits to certain areas. Cities that rely on tourism to sustain their economies, like New York City, Miami in Florida, and San Francisco or Los Angeles in California may suffer economic loss during periods of gun violence, especially if tourists are harmed.

An additional intangible cost to society is the fear that firearms convey to people. When large numbers of people have concealed weapons permits, residents cannot feel safe knowing that there are many around them that are armed and could use their weapon at any time, particularly in those states with Stand Your Ground Laws. This creates an atmosphere of distrust and suspicion towards others and does nothing to improve societal relations.

As with injuries to the victims, communities are not compensated by the firearm industry or its satellites and consumers for the increased risks they face.

The Cost of Protecting Our Leaders

There is also a cost to society of protecting high profile figures such as the President, Vice President, and members of Congress. In the case of the President and Vice President, millions of dollars are expended on ensuring their safety from harm, arming and housing members of the Secret Service, and limiting their access to the public. Society suffers from the lack of interaction with their Commander in Chief and pays for protection through their taxes. While they need protection regardless of the prevalence of firearms, the ubiquity of firearms increases the risks to their lives, as witness the assassinations of President John F. Kennedy, his brother Robert and icons like Martin Luther King and Medger Evers.

Had Lee Harvey Oswald not been able to procure a rifle as easily as he did, John Kennedy might be alive today. Had Sirhan Sirhan not been able to obtain a revolver, Robert could be alive today. We place our leaders in extreme jeopardy with our attitude to firearms.

Benefits of Reducing Gun Violence

If every U.S. state were as peaceful as Maine, the estimated reduced costs of violent crime would generate $274 Billion in extra economic savings[110]. The increase in economic activity could potentially produce over 1.7 million jobs. Raising minimum wages, creating jobs for poorer Americans, and ridding the country of firearms could generate $2.7 Trillion in new economic activity. The reluctance of conservatives to consider economic stimulus as part of the solution to gun crime and crime in general is costing the country dearly in both economic activity and lives lost. The estimated total cost of violence to the U.S. is $460 Billion, while lost productivity amounts to $318 Billion each year.

If gun violence is reduced by concerted gun regulation in particularly violent areas of the country, it is quite likely that property values would rise accordingly. This gives members of the community, and by extension, the entire nation an extra economic incentive to introduce gun restrictions. People who own homes in the affected areas could well see price appreciation in their properties, that would enable them to move up the social ladder and further mitigate gun violence. There is a causal link between poverty, unemployment and gun violence, so any increase in assets would likely lead to a decrease in such violence.

The relative cost of policing those violent areas could well pay for itself in increased economic activity, as well as a reduction in deaths. Gun violence costs society in increased taxation, deteriorating property values, limited choices in domicile and concerns about personal safety. There are increased policing costs, criminal justice, and hospitalization for victims, funeral costs and possible medical costs throughout life for survivors. There is an economic cost to children growing up in violent areas, where schoolwork and attendance may suffer. Young children can be pressed to join gangs, contributing to societal breakdown.

Cost to Society in Lives Lost

There is a cost to society of the gun lobby clinging to their Second Amendment rights without considering the ramifications of those rights. Consider that in 2011, 32,163 people died from gunshot wounds and 73,883 were wounded. That means that 30% of people shot died from their wounds, an unacceptably high number.

The cost for African Americans and Hispanics is particularly severe. The homicide rate for African American men is 2.4 times higher than it is for Hispanics and 15.3 times higher than that for non-Hispanic white males. The probability of a black man being lost to gun violence is 62% higher than the chance of them dying in a motor vehicle accident. For black youth, there is a 1 in 115 chance of being killed by gunfire by age 20. In comparison, for white youths, there is only a 1 in 512 chance of being killed[111]. If non-fatal injuries are considered, there is a 1 in 20 chance that an African American male will be shot by the age of 20.

The relative risks of death resulting from firearms as opposed to knife wounds are stark. In the U.S., a single death results from every five people hospitalized with firearms injuries, whereas for cut/stab wounds, one death results from every 759 injuries[112]. If every single firearm injury were replaced with a knife injury, the resulting death toll would be far lower, as would the resulting costs. A gunshot injury in the U.S. can cost up to 50 times what a stabbing injury costs.

Jeff Cooper, board member of the NRA in 2000, had this to say about the prevalence of firearm death among economically disadvantaged populations[113],

> "The consensus is that no more than 5 to 10 people in 100 who die by gunfire in Los Angeles are any loss to society. These people [the other 95%] fight small wars among themselves. It would seem a valid social service to keep them well supplied with ammunition."

Gun violence disproportionately targets people of color, for reasons related predominantly to their economically disadvantaged status. Murder and manslaughter victims are far more likely to be African-American or Latino. African-Americans constitute 13% of the U.S. population, but suffer 56% of all firearm homicides[114]. The death rate among African Americans is 16.3, ranking with poor undeveloped nations, while among whites it is 2.2[115]. The gun lobby continues to show a callous disregard for the suffering of those communities and those lost and a lack of empathy for the victims.

Risk to Populations with Criminal Records

Access to firearms exacerbates violence among populations with prior criminal records. In Philadelphia between 1985 and 1996 gun homicides in those populations increased from 73% to 93%[116]. In Boston between 1990 and 1994, 75% of homicide victims under 21 had a previous criminal record. By these measures, firearms are more dangerous to criminals than they are to other members of the public[117]. This shows that background checks must prevent felons from obtaining firearms, whether on the retail market or on the secondary market.

Risk to the Poor

A higher risk of gun shot injury and death is present among the poor, the less educated, the mentally ill or those involved in crime, demonstrating the effect that inequities have on society. For many people, the lower rates of firearm injury among average Americans leads them to believe that the problem can be ignored, since they do not routinely happen in their neighborhoods, as well as ridding the population of those they consider undesirable.

As with so many aspects of American society, the poor are disproportionately affected by gun violence. A study found that 79% of gunshot victims in greater Nashville were Medicaid recipients, compared with 45% for all other emergency room patients. African Americans were three times more likely to be gunshot victims than were whites[118]. They were also more likely to be male (87.5%). Black patients between the ages of 18 and 25 were far more likely to be victims of gun violence than were their white counterparts. Even when accounting for socioeconomic status, the rate of victimization among blacks was 75.8 per 100,000 compared to 2.6 for whites and 6.1 for Latinos.

Residents of poverty-stricken communities, especially predominantly African American neighborhoods, are aware of the enormous burden that freely available firearms have. Residents of those communities have a far greater probability of being killed by firearm than those in more affluent communities. This leads African Americans to favor gun regulation over gun rights (68% to 42%), whereas white communities that are not as affected by violence favor gun rights (51% to 42%)[119]. The causes of this violence have much to do with disparities in nutrition, prenatal health, parenting skills, health care and education rather than an innate proclivity for violence.

Since gun violence in poorer communities does not have a direct impact on the more affluent areas of the country, those communities with violence are dismissed as not affecting the lives of the affluent. The affluent cushion themselves within their suburbs and gated communities instead of understanding that gun violence can spill over into their areas. Arming themselves does not alleviate the problem, rather it is likely to worsen gun violence as firearms go missing, are stolen, or are redirected by unscrupulous arms dealers to poorer areas.

The Dreaded Handgun

Between 1996 and 1998, for a young person under 20, there was one death by firearm for every 4.4 visits to an emergency room. For injuries other than firearms, the ratio was 1:760. The increase in youth crime corresponded with the entry of semi-automatic weapons into the market in the late 1980's, actively encouraged and promoted by the gun industry. These weapons hold more ammunition, have higher calibers and are thus far more lethal than ever before.

According to the ATF, by 1999, half of all weapons recovered after the commission of a crime were semi-automatics. This also brought increases in firearm violence, higher numbers of bullet wounds and a higher proportion of fatalities[120]. The growing importance of youth gangs only exacerbated this situation, causing more guns to flood the streets. The entire increase in homicides during those years can be traced to violence committed by youths with firearms. Youths acquire firearms through family, friends, straw purchases or theft. The proximate cause of the change was not a shift in youth personality, but the ready availability of semi-automatic firearms.

Firearms account for 70% of murders in the U.S., while handguns account for 50% of all murders. Far from most murders being committed during the commission of a felony, only 14% of murders occur during the commission of a felony, while 21% occur during an argument, many of which would probably not be fatal for participants were it not for the presence of firearms[121].

The Family cost of Firearm Ownership

In light of all the gun violence in the USA, I'd prefer my democracy unleaded
(Jayseth Guberman*)*

Few people who own firearms understand the risks involved to those around them, including their spouses, children, friends and other members of the community. In part because of the Supreme Court decision in *Heller* that people have the right to own firearms in the home, but also because of the prevailing gun culture and the gun lobby, society is forced to endure the presence of firearms and their accompanying violent death and injury. Many people in a household have no choice as to whether to live in a home with a firearm, especially women and children, who are often not given a vote in the matter. Yet, they are disproportionately affected by gun violence in the home since men and adults are more likely to own firearms.

Redefining Childhood

In the book "Gun Control" from the Opposing Viewpoints series[122], Wayne Lapierre decries the use of the term "child" when discussing gun violence. His claim is that children should be defined as those below fourteen years of age, which then allows him to claim that there are a greater number of deaths from drowning than from firearms. He goes further than this to claim that there are so few deaths of children from firearm accidents that we can effectively discount them as a cause of death. He also goes so far as to compare the number of drownings of toddlers with gun accidents. Most lucid people would agree that toddlers should not be around firearms; even the NRA should be able to see the sense in that.

Accidental death is not the only way children under 14 lose their lives to firearms. Homicide and suicide are also causes of premature death. While there may be more deaths from drowning, children are around various bodies of water every day throughout their lives, leaving much room for accidental death. The same cannot be said for firearms. Most responsible adults ensure that children do not have access to firearms at any point in their youth, for good reason.

If we were to define "child" as anyone below eighteen years of age, the age of majority, the ratio between drowning deaths and gun deaths changes markedly. Twice the number of minors dies from firearms as from drowning. The same is true for stabbings, falls, suffocation or physical blows, all of which are exceeded by gun deaths.

If we compare the number of homicides by firearm and drowning among minors, there are 38 times more firearm homicides than drowning homicides. Accidental deaths happen because we are human. Firearm homicides are almost entirely preventable through the introduction of stringent firearm restrictions.

Increasing the Risk of Death and Injury in the Home

Having a firearm in the home sharply increases the risk of injury or death, whether self-inflicted or caused by a household member. This risk is demonstrably higher than the odds of killing an intruder in self-defense. The risks to every member of the household are far greater than for households that do not have firearms. This alone is reason enough to have no firearms in a home. The presence of firearms in the home allows people to commit acts of violence that are far more likely to be fatal than violent acts committed without firearms. It is also more efficient and more successful to attempt suicide with a firearm than any other method. The possible benefits of firearm presence in the home are heavily outweighed by the detriments of their presence in almost every scenario. There is little if any credible, empirical evidence that firearms in the home provide a deterrent to injury during break-ins or altercations.

A study in the American Journal of Epidemiology found that at least 42% of homicides and three quarters of suicides occur in homes with firearms. At least 76% of homicides are by people we know, not by criminals[123]. There is little doubt, given the many studies done on firearms in the home, that having a firearm in the home dramatically increases the risks of violent death. The research found that people living in homes with firearms were 1.9 times more likely to die from homicide than those without[124]. They were also at increased risk of dying from firearm homicide than those without. Those living in homes with firearms were 31.1 times more likely to die from firearm suicide than any other method. The risks of a male dying from suicide were 10.4 times greater than for males in homes without guns. The study also found that regardless of the number or type of firearm, whether handgun or long gun, or where or how they were stored, suicide risk was dramatically higher. No variable other than firearm presence was predictive of firearm homicide.

A 1992 study published in the New England Journal of Medicine found that the presence of a firearm in the home was associated with a five times greater risk of death by suicide and three times greater risk of homicide[125]. A 2003 paper found that the risk of homicide in homes with firearms was 1.72 times greater than in homes without firearms, and suicide risks 16.89 times greater than in homes without firearms[126]. A report in 1993 on gun ownership concluded that rather than provide protection for members of a household, guns are associated with an increased homicide risk by a "family member or intimate acquaintance"[127]. There is little reason to believe that these risks have changed in the interim.

Research by Arthur Kellerman of Emory University conducted in Kings County, Washington determined that more than half of all fatal shootings occurred in the home. Of the 395 fatalities investigated, 333 were suicides, 41 criminal homicides, 12 accidental deaths, while only nine were legally justifiable homicides[128]. Justifiable homicides, including incidents in which firearms were used to stop an intruder constituted only 2% of the total fatalities. Accidental deaths alone accounted for 3% of fatalities, while homicide accounted for 10% of deaths. Suicide was a particular risk for residents at 84%. The presence of firearms was far more dangerous to the inhabitants of the home than to intruders or other self-defense uses.

A gun in the home is 22 times more likely to be used in an unintentional shooting, criminal assault, homicide or attempted or completed suicide than to be used to injure or kill in self defense[129]. A recent article describes how a gun in the home is twelve times more likely to kill a member of the household than an intruder[130]. Guns in the home are correlated with a five times greater risk of intimate partner homicide and an increased risk of injury and death of children.

The risks of a child between 5 and 14 years of age dying accidentally by firearm in the home are 13 times higher than for other industrialized nations, while the rate of firearm homicide for youths 15 to 24 are 43 times higher according to another analysis. Given that people regularly become involved in violent incidents, the presence of a firearm dangerously increases the risk of death[131].

All violent or criminal interactions become far more dangerous when firearms are involved, making common "quarrels, disputes, assaults and robberies more deadly"[132]. Disputes within the family can more quickly lead to fatalities over such mundane issues as money, matters of the heart or domestic problems. The presence of alcohol only exacerbates the situation, widening the circle of possible fatalities to friends and neighbors.

The threat of home invasion as a cause of homicide is far less than the risk of death from a relative or acquaintance. Research published in the American Journal of Epidemiology concluded that at least 76.3% of homicide victims knew their assailant, who was either a family member or intimate acquaintance[133]. Almost one third of all homicides happened during an argument within the family, fifteen percent during robbery, four percent during a drug deal and forty four percent for other reasons. Men were at greater risk of suicide by firearm than were women, but women in homes with firearms were 2.3 times more likely to die by firearm than homes without. In addition, most female firearm fatalities were in the home, as were homicides involving children and the elderly[134].

The likelihood that a firearm will be used to perpetrate senseless acts of violence or stupidity when there is a firearm in the home is far higher than for homes without firearms. By way of comparison, the successful use of a firearm in self-defense in the home is rare and difficult to accomplish, given the logistical problems, and the element of surprise. Studies claim that successful defensive firearm use in home invasions is about 1%, and 0.1% for sexual assault[135]. According to law enforcement reports, most uses of firearms even in these cases were inappropriate and probably unlawful. A firearm in the home is far more likely to be used for violence, suicide or accident than self-defense.

Prof. David Hemenway wrote the following[136],

> Regular citizens with guns, who are sometimes tired, angry, drunk or afraid, and who are not trained in dispute resolution, have lots of opportunities for inappropriate gun use. People engage in innumerable annoying and somewhat hostile interactions with each other in the course of a lifetime"

People who are inadequately trained in the law, or in law enforcement procedures are thus far more likely to take action that is not warranted, to injure innocent bystanders, or to engage in potentially fatal firearm use against friends, spouses, neighbors or others. Firearms make a home a far more hostile and dangerous place to live. Given the heightened risks of a firearm in the home to the occupants, it is irrational to retain firearms for defensive purposes.

Due to the systematic obstruction by the gun lobby and Congress of research into firearm injuries and deaths, there are insufficient studies of significant size that can be used to indisputably demonstrate the correlation between firearms in the home and injuries. As an example, in a state like South Dakota, by law, death certificates cannot be used as a basis for research, despite the positive social value of such research.

The Failure of Parental Responsibility

Parents who are both gun owners and have children in the home have a special responsibility to ensure that those children do not have any access to those firearms. They should ensure that the firearms are properly secured, ammunition is kept separate from the firearms, firearms have trigger locks and other safety features, and children are expressly forbidden from handling said firearms without trained supervision. Education alone is insufficient, since some research has determined that the education of children regarding improper handling of firearms is often ineffective.

The General Accounting Office found that 31% of unintentional gun fatalities in 10 cities may have been avoided through the use of child safety devices, including safety grips, magazine disconnect devices and trigger locks, and loaded chamber indicators[137]. New technologies such as personalized firearms would go a long way to preventing unauthorized people from using firearms. The gun lobby, instead of insisting on the paramount importance of children's safety claims that locking up guns *"renders homeowners defenseless and gives criminals a clear advantage in home invasions, and renders firearms useless in self-defense situations."*

Far from locking firearms away from children, firearm instructor Rob Pincus argued that the best place to keep a firearm is in a child's bedroom. He claims [138]

> "If you are worried that your kid is going to try and break into the safe that is in their bedroom with a gun in it, you have bigger problems than home defense. If I am going to go to the kid anyway and I have an extra gun and an extra safe, why not put it in their closet?"

While it may be a parent's natural instinct to run to their child's room in the unlikely event of a home invasion, it is the child's instinct to investigate everything around him. An inquisitive child will find a way into a gun safe, which is far easier if the safe is in his room than in the parents' room. The lack of responsibility on the part of the parent can lead all too easily to vicarious culpability in the event of the accidental death or injury of the child or others.

We also have to consider the safety of children who are only visiting; these children should not be subject to the dictates of the homeowner. Their parents have the right to determine whether their children are safe in the homes of others. It is difficult for parents, and often impractical to ensure that the homes to which their children go have secured their firearms.

The most effective way to keep the home a safer place for children is to remove all firearms from the premises. Without firearms in the home, there are fewer opportunities for accidents or violence to take lives. There ought to be special restrictions on homes with children put in place by Congress to ensure that children cannot be harmed with firearms; this should include a complete ban on weapons in homes with children or confiscation of weapons. This is particularly true in homes in which one or more individuals have a history of violence or spousal or child abuse. Alternatively, firearms should be properly secured and stiff penalties imposed in the absence of adherence to these rules.

Ultimately, parents are in part to blame for the massacres that continue to occur around the country. Unlike the gun lobby, which becomes animated and circles the wagons to safeguard its putative right to guns, many parents are complacent spectators in the gun wars, ceding ground to the gun extremists rather than taking up the banner for their children. Some parents seem more preoccupied with paying the mortgage or the grocery bill than they are with the safety of their children. This is why the gun lobby wins every battle and overcomes every burden to stand for what they believe in. Parents should do be allowed to do what they need to do to safeguard their children from assault weapons and the arms trade. Our Constitution was not so enshrined as to protect the right to own firearms over and above the rights of children to life and safety. Parents and society have ceded the battleground to the gun lobby without fully understanding the risks to their families and communities.

While many parents are to blame for the deaths of so many children, they cannot be entirely personally responsible for the safety of their children. Society has an important part to play. The gun lobby would have us believe that parents must shoulder the entire burden of a safer society, a pipe dream in a large, complex society. It is up to that society to ensure the safety of its residents, to take guns off the street and from the homes of those who are incapable of responsible behavior.

Parental Fantasies Concerning Their Children and Guns

Far too many parents believe that their children would not touch a firearm, or would inform an adult if they found a gun. In a study of children 8 to 12 left in a room with two toy guns and one real firearm, children of parents who thought their sons had little interest in guns handled the firearms 65% of the time. Thirty-five percent of boys thought to have a low interest in firearms actually pulled the trigger[139]. Education programs for children aimed at reducing firearm injuries do not have their intended effect and may actually exacerbate the situation by increasing the child's desire to handle firearms.

One study determined that 39% of children knew the location of parents' guns and 22% had handled them despite parents reporting otherwise[140]. Children under 10 were just as likely to report knowing where guns were kept and handling them as were older children. Children educated through gun safety programs were no less likely to handle firearms than those without access to these classes.

A study concerning teenagers with suicidal tendencies found that of parents counseled to remove firearms from the home, only 27% complied, while 17% of parents who did not have firearms acquired them in the two years following counseling[141]. These two studies show that many parents are either incapable of acting responsibly or are misguided in their approach to children and firearms. Far from protecting their families, they are dramatically increasing the risks to their families when they allow firearms in the home.

The Psychological Cost of Gun Violence for Victims

Little available data highlights the psychological costs of gun violence on victims, their families and the broader communities that surround them. The fear of gun violence in certain communities is sufficient to prohibit the free movement of people around those communities, the free association with others, or the free exercise of social or commercial activities. People may have an inordinate fear of straying from their apartments or homes because of the dangers of gun violence.

Concerns about gun violence affect attitudes to safety, about raising taxes to cover costs, and severely limits choices especially for the poor about where to live, work, travel and which schools children should attend. Reduced gun violence permits communities to exist without adapting behavior to account for the firearm threat. Individuals can travel freely, create businesses, or work without fear of violence.

Guns are used not purely as defensive weapons, they are used to coerce, intimidate, to injure and assault and to keep women subjugated to males or the vulnerable to the armed. Some communities experience endemic intimidation of women and children with the threat of firearms. That fear can well transmit to men in the community, through fear for their families and their own safety.

The use of firearms as a form of coercion in violent domestic relationships is well documented. Women especially may be fearful of harm to their children, pets, siblings, parents or others by spouses, gangs, or others who use firearms to intimidate. The display or visible cleaning of a firearm can well serve as a warning to vulnerable or abused women.

Children, especially vulnerable to violence in their communities may experience psychological trauma that affects their mental and psychological development, aggression against others and socially aberrant behavior, imposing additional unnecessary costs on society.

The ruling by the Supreme Court permitting the ownership of firearms by all residents imposes an unwarranted cost on communities. Non-gun owners must now be concerned that those around them are armed, especially with highly destructive firearms. Given a choice, people might choose to reside in communities where guns are not permitted, but the courts have seized that option from them and increased their level of anxiety, and tangible risk. Many people see an surge in gun ownership as a threat to their communities, and now the Roberts' court has imposed it on them with their interpretation of the Second Amendment. This imperious act sacrifices the security of the majority for the annexed freedoms of a minority.

Giving Children Access to Firearms

The gun culture has a particularly detrimental effect on children. In a society in which there are 300m largely unregulated guns, it is all too easy for youths to obtain firearms. While other weapons may cause injury and death, none are capable of the efficient lethality of firearms, especially in the hands of youths. Death and injury are more frequent and more frequently fatal with firearms than are injuries with knives, clubs or fists. Given the youthful propensity for impulsive acts, an argument can escalate quickly to violence, with firearms dramatically raising the risk of fatalities.

The Appalling Toll of Firearms on Children

In 2010, 2,711 children and teens died because of gun violence[142]. Every three hours, one young life is lost to firearms. In 2006, 63 preschoolers under five years of age were murdered with a firearm, exceeding the 48 law enforcement officers killed in the line of duty[143]. By 2010, that figure had risen sharply to 82 preschool deaths. American youth under 15 commit suicide at eleven times the rate experienced in other developed countries combined, while the overall suicide rate is twice that of other countries[144].

In 2010, firearms injured 15,576 children and teenagers[145], a 29% increase on the number injured in 2003, the year before the Assault Weapons Ban expired[146]. By 2011, that figure rose to 16,700 injured youths. One child dies or is injured every 30 minutes, while 50 children and teens die or are injured each day. According to the National Association of School Psychologists, of the children aged 10-19 murdered in 2010, 84% were killed with a firearm[147].

The 1994 World Development Report reports that American children under the age of 15 were 12 times more likely to be killed by a firearm than were children in 25 other industrialized nations combined, while the firearm homicide rate was 16 times higher[148]. Yet, if gun suicides were excluded, the suicide rate among children would be similar to that of other countries[149]. In 1999, guns in the home were used 72% of the time when children are accidentally killed, injured or committed suicide with a firearm[150]. Based on a 2004 study published in the National Medical Association Journal, in Washington D.C., the risk of a child being a victim of a major gunshot wound or stabbing rose sharply at age 14 and continued to rise strongly until the age of 18[151]. This echoes the results of similar studies from around the nation.

Over the past thirty years, guns were used to murder four times more children than any other method including stabbing, strangling or drowning[152]. In 2009, 84.5% of homicides of people 15 to 19 were firearm related. Firearm homicide rates for youths 15 to 24 were 35.7 times higher than other high-income countries[153]. The American Academy of Pediatrics (AAP) has lobbied Congress to tighten gun laws to combat gun violence[154]. The gun lobby actively seeks to disparage and undermine the efforts of the AAP, working with legislators to impede the groups' scientific research into gun violence[155].

Firearm homicide is the second leading cause of death among young people ages 15-24 after unintentional accidents such as motor vehicle crashes. More than four thousand youths died from gun homicides in 2007, along with almost 2000 suicides by gun[156]. In 2008, firearms were the leading cause of death for children aged 10-14 in at least six states, California, Alaska, Louisiana, Maryland, Nevada and Virginia[157]. While the rates of motor vehicle death for youths under 20 have declined from 9.8 to 5.3 since 1999, gun death rates have barely budged, declining from 4.2 to 3.2.

Marian Wright Edelman of the Children's Defense Fund, asserts that 2,694 children and teens were killed by guns in 2010. Of those, 1,773 were victims of homicide, and 67 were elementary school children. Since 1979, 119,079 children and teens have been killed by gunfire[158]. This is rapidly approaching the total number of Americans killed in battle in World War I (53,402), Vietnam (47,434), the Korean War (33,739), and the Iraq war (3,517) combined. For children in some parts of America, this nation has become a war zone, except that it is more dangerous for children to live in some parts of this nation than it is in many war zones. The inner cities and poorer areas of this nation, like South Chicago, New Orleans, Washington D.C and Baltimore, are particularly hazardous for children.

The Danger of Guns In The Child's Home

Like alcohol, drugs and other dangerous items, firearms and children do not mix well. In homes with firearms, children become comfortable with the idea of being around firearms, which can lull them into a false sense of security and the erroneous belief that firearms are safe. Yet, their risk of injury or death is far higher once a firearm is introduced to the home.

In 2000, 22 million children (34%) lived in homes with guns[159]. In 69% of those homes, there were multiple firearms[160]. Fewer than half of the households (39%) with children and firearms stored their firearms unloaded, locked and separate from ammunition. Another survey determined that only 30% to 39% of gun owning households in the U.S. store their firearms unlocked and unloaded[161]. Preschoolers aged 0-4 were 17 times more likely to die from a gun accident in those states with the most guns compared to those with the least, while children aged 5-14 were 13 times more likely to die[162]. Guns stored loaded and unlocked are most likely to be found in the South, in homes with teenagers and in homes with at least one household member in law enforcement.

The gun lobby claims that gun owners are responsible, and yet those owners are not storing firearms away from children. Children are inquisitive, and even when told not to touch firearms, their natural curiosity is likely to overcome those instructions. Children also have friends and neighbors that are not privy to those instructions, and who may be present in the home. Teenagers with suicidal tendencies are even less likely to obey these instructions, and unsecured firearms give them the means and opportunity to take their own lives.

Children demonstrate an inability to judge their risk of injury, identify hazardous conditions or apply classroom lessons to real life situations. They will ignore instructions not to interact or play with firearms and display aggressive behavior when interacting with firearms[163]. Teenagers are cognitively more mature in their understanding of gun safety, but they have more trouble assessing the very real risk of injury to themselves and others than do adults. They are also more likely to submit to peer pressure and engage in risky behavior or acts of braggadocio[164]. Teenagers are also far more likely to carry firearms if their peers are already carrying.

The Traumatic Impact of Firearms on Children

Children are particularly adversely affected by gun violence through loss of a parent, sibling or other loved one. They are also affected by gun violence in other ways. Firearm injury disproportionately affects young people between 15 and 24, with homicide the second leading cause of death after motor vehicle accidents, and suicide third. Among black youth, gun homicide is the leading cause of death[165]. According to research published in the New England Journal of Medicine, guns kill twice as many children and teenagers as does cancer, five times more than heart disease and 15 times more than infection[166]. While we as a nation research and treat other serious health risks, we do nothing to mitigate the firearm tragedy among our youth.

The death of a parent, a sibling, or a friend has a dramatic impact on children, who are most impressionable at a young age. The impact of gun violence on children is also long lasting. Domestic abuse or violence, and parents with substance abuse issues can have a powerful emotional impact on a child's development and health. The effects of being exposed to incessant violence include depression, posttraumatic stress, anxiety, dissociation and aggression[167].

This exposure need not be direct, but may be experienced in schools, the wider community or through the media. Exposure to violence also leads to anger, disturbed sleep and poor performance in schools, or risky behaviors such as drug abuse or sexual experimentation, further exacerbating the obstacles faced by youth in poorer, violence prone districts. This can lead to higher levels of violence among youth, and creates a cycle of violence that can be difficult to break.

A study of seven year olds living in inner Philadelphia determined that 75% had heard gunfire, one third saw someone get shot and 10% lived in a household in which someone had been shot or stabbed[168]. These children experienced more anxiety, depression, low self-esteem, low grades and more school truancy. Over 60% of these children were concerned that they might be killed, and 19%

sometimes wished they were dead. Few of these young children receive any treatment for psychological trauma.

Guns in The Classroom

Violence in school is of particular concern, given the exposure of large numbers of children and teens to that violence. However, despite the concerns, schools are among the safest places in the nation for children. The probability of a student being a victim of homicide while at school was about 1 in 2.5 million, whereas the chance of a student being killed in a motor vehicle accident is 1 in 16,000[169].

The very idea of putting armed guards in schools considering how safe they are is expensive, unnecessary and does nothing to mitigate student firearm deaths, which mostly occur outside schools. The massacre in Newtown was caused by access to firearms in the home, not because schools are vulnerable. Children in high-risk areas would be far safer from firearm homicide if access to firearms in society were to be reduced.

The Youth Gun Culture

Some weapons not considered dangerous to children, can have a profound impact on their lives. A simple pellet or BB gun can cause significant damage, and not just to vulnerable organs like the eye. One study of injuries caused by these weapons found perforations of the stomach, liver and pancreas requiring abdominal exploration[170]. Some parents give these weapons to children to use unsupervised without understanding the dangers involved both to their children and to the wider community. These weapons are also used to target vulnerable cats and dogs, as well as squirrels, birds and other neighborhood wildlife. Even more disturbing is that parents allow weapons that are more deadly around children.

An increasing number of youths are carrying firearms illegally. In 1997, 1 in 7 male juveniles reported carrying a firearm outside the home[171]. This problem is most severe in dangerous and disadvantaged inner cities where crime and violence are more common. In one study of 758 school children, 22% claimed to carry firearms[172]. In addition,

88% of convicted juvenile offenders reported carrying weapons[173]. An estimated 51% of guns used in crimes by juveniles and people between 18 and 24 are acquired by "Straw purchasers", people who buy several legal guns through dealers, and sell them to criminals, violent offenders and children[174].

In another investigation, among youths who carried guns 48% were given or loaned the weapon by a friend of family member, 35% purchased the weapon illegally, 5% received the weapon through a straw purchase and 6% stole or traded something for the weapon[175]. A small percentage of gun dealers will sell firearms illegally to youths. Guns sold by 1.2% of dealers account for 57% of guns later traced by ATF following a crime[176]. Of those teens that carry concealed weapons, more than 90% have been victimized, more than 90% had witnessed violence and 73% had a family member who had been shot[177].

Studies show that many children involved in gangs and gun violence are involved in this life only reluctantly. If reasonable curbs on the availability of firearms were introduced, the tensions involved in high crime areas would diminish and reduce the lethality of violent confrontations[178]. Studies suggest that police pressure on youths and gangs can reduce the risks of gun possession and of fatal shootings.

A Child's Right to Self-Defense

The primary reason given by adolescents for carrying concealed weapons is self-defense, which is directly related to the conditions in which they live[179]. Children and teens that do not feel safe and secure in their neighborhoods are far more likely to carry concealed weapons. It is only when states and cities take action to make communities safer by reducing gun availability and economically empower residents, that youths will feel safe enough not to carry firearms.

The refusal to remove firearms from economically stressed communities or stimulate the economies of economically depressed cities ultimately leads to more crime, more violence and more gun deaths. The temptation to deal with youth violence by incarcerating offenders is like spreading skin lotion on smallpox, it may provide some temporary relief, but the patient will eventually die from the lack of appropriate treatment.

Youth, Guns and The City Life

In Chicago, more than 4,000 people have been shot in the last four years. During 2008, 510 people were murdered, 80% by gunfire. Nearly half were between the ages of 10 and 25, and mostly male[180]. Children in some areas of the city can no longer go out into their front garden or playgrounds to play because of the fear of being shot[181]. The mayor of Chicago wants to treat guns like cars, and have registration, but the gun lobby is opposing this measure out of concern for the rights of citizens. It is striking that the gun lobby does not consider the rights of Chicago's children. The right of the people, especially children, to be safe in their own homes, appears to be a right Illinois will not recognize. The report on Chicago demonstrates that we have made far more progress in understanding how to protect the public from every threat to life other than gun violence.

The increasing firearm possession by young drug dealers causes other young people to carry firearms as protection. This was particularly true during the crack cocaine epidemic in the 1980's. Gang involvement is related to the failure of the social system to provide youths with a safe environment and social opportunities. The gang fills the social deficit imposed by a failing school system and reduced opportunities for parents.

One in five youths killed by gunfire in Chicago was either an innocent bystander, or not the intended victim of the shooter. Merely being in the wrong place at the wrong time can be lethal for children. Father Michael Pfleger of St. Sabina's Roman Catholic Church in Chicago has parishioners advising college students not to return to Chicago during the summer of 2012 because of the violence in that city[182]. The increases in gun violence appear to have something to do with the high level of unemployment, failing schools and program cutbacks due to budgetary constraints. By this measure, if extreme budget cutbacks as proposed in the 2013 Congressional Sequester are fully implemented, the number of gun deaths, especially among youths, is likely to rise commensurately.

How Guns Destroy Childhood

The impact on the community is not limited to physical victims. The fear of death pervades the community and the families of those victims. Rather than being fully participating members of a community, children no longer play with one another, and are driven to and from school, or the corner store. Children and parents live in fear of groups of young men on street corners. A study by Cullen and Levitt, estimates that every homicide reduces a city's population[183]. Jens Ludwig, director of the University of Chicago Crime Lab states that each homicide in Chicago reduces the city's population by 70 people[184].

Like Candy to Toddlers: Selling Firearms to Children

The gun lobby seems to do it's utmost to exacerbate gun injuries. The gun industry is boosting sales of firearms by advertising to children as young as five years old. In Kentucky, the ramifications of this are becoming clearer after the accidental shooting death of two-year-old Caroline Sparks by her five-year-old brother Kristian with his own gun, a Crickett rifle[185]. This weapon is marketed specifically to young children to encourage entry into the world of gun possession, just as a cocaine dealer will give children a sample to get them addicted to hard drugs. While the tobacco industry implicitly markets their deadly products to children, society cannot countenance actions of this type; the gun industry is no different from the alcohol or drug industry. Their watchword is profit at any price. Kentucky, lacking responsible gun laws, is unlikely to charge the parents with this child's' death, despite their reckless behavior.

We do not allow anyone under age 18 to drive, or anyone under 21 to purchase alcohol; children are not yet sufficiently mature to understand the consequences of their actions, or make adult decisions. Giving a rifle as a gift to a five-year-old child ought to be seen as child abuse, which has already cost at least one life. The arms industry profits by marketing deadly weapons to children. Residents of the town in which Caroline died consider that her death is no-ones business but theirs, but government has a compelling interest in protecting the vulnerable. The two-year-old girl had no protection from her grandmother's actions, no say in the matter, which cost her life. The community has an obligation to ensure that deaths like this do not happen; to that extent, Kentucky and its residents are to blame. The child should never have been alone with the firearm; to give the rifle as a gift is reprehensible.

The Crickett Company markets their product intensively to children. The owners should be held to account for the company's actions. The company claims that it made over 60,000 Crickett rifles in 2008[186], causing the unnecessary death of tens of thousands of animals. There is no compelling reason for the massacre of large numbers of animals, merely to entertain the nations youth. Tradition is no compelling reason to own destructive weapons; as society advances, we understand that many of the things we once did as a nation are no longer warranted, and we change our ways. Giving guns to children is a tradition that society cannot countenance and ought to be abolished, as we did with cigarette smoking and alcohol for youths.

Many of the shooting incidents in which children accidentally take their own lives occur during shooting outings with the family. Despite being with experienced shooters and instructed by those shooters, accidents still take these young lives and place the lives of others at risk. The mistake is placing firearms in the hands of children who should have no part of handling firearms. Yet, the shooting lifestyle for children is actively encouraged by the gun lobby.

How Guns Enable Suicide at Home

Introducing a firearm into the home immediately makes suicide far simpler to accomplish than any other method.

The risks of suicide in homes with guns are as high as 10 times that in homes without firearms. The risk is higher for all occupants of a home with a firearm, including children and the spouse, and not just the owner. Among Americans younger than 40, suicide is the second leading cause of death. Of all suicides completed each year, more than half were committed with a firearm[187]. Most suicide attempts are impulsive, made in the heat of a crisis and possession of a firearm is more likely to result in a successful attempt. Once a person has had time to think about their situation, it may not appear as dire as first imagined. This is one reason that waiting periods are so crucial in preventing unnecessary death.

Suicides are a particular risk to the elderly white population, while fatalities among men outnumber those for women at least four to one. More than 90% of suicide victims suffer from some form of mental illness, including alcoholism, schizophrenia and drug addiction.

The correlation holds true even when accounting for region, states and urban areas. The same is true when controlling for SMI (Serious Mental Illness), alcohol abuse, drug abuse, unemployment, and poverty level. In comparison, the non-firearm suicide rate is unaffected by gun prevalence[188]. Each day 46 Americans commit suicide with a firearm, including 2 teenagers and 3.5 young adults. Gun prevalence in the home presents particularly acute risks for adolescents and young adults. Of the people who take their own lives, experts estimate that no more than 10% to 15% are determined to commit suicide. Of people who survive suicide, only 10% make another successful attempt. Access to a firearm usually guarantees the success of a suicide attempt.

The decline in gun ownership in the 1990's coincided with a similar fall in firearm suicide rates, while the non-firearm suicide rate remained constant. The proportion of Americans considering suicide during this period did not change. While it is feasible that people with suicidal inclinations are more likely to have a firearm in the home, studies do not accord with that view[189].

Even mandating that firearms be locked and ammunition kept separately may reduce suicide risks. In the *Heller* case, the Supreme Court ruled that the Washington D.C. law requiring that firearms be secured was unconstitutional, ensuring that homes with firearms would experience higher suicide death rates. However, this increase is slight; the mere presence of firearms in the home is a far more compelling risk for suicide. There was no compelling evidence that the Courts' ruling increased the incidence of legally justifiable self-defense.

Increasing Risk for African Americans

In a black home with two male children, given the firearm death rates in 1998, the probability that a mother would lose one of her children to gunfire was 1 in 115, with the greatest risk stemming from homicide. For whites, that number was 1 in 512, with much of the risk stemming from suicide. There is little reason to believe that these statistics have changed much in the ensuing years. In 1998, African American males aged 15 to 19 died by firearm homicide at a rate of 63 in 100,000[190]. That rate is higher than the overall firearm death rate in every country in Central America in 2005[191].

The difference in rates of violence between African Americans, Hispanics and whites are explained by parents' marital status, how recently parents immigrated (recent immigrants are less likely to commit violent acts), and where they live. Rates of violence in a child's community and conditions in the neighborhood are strongly correlated with the child's chances of committing violent acts.

American Children Die at a Greater Rate Than Other Developed Nations

Taking 23 of the world's wealthiest nations into consideration, 87% of children killed by guns are American. In 2002, the firearm related death rate among youth under 15 was 16 times higher than 25 other industrialized nations combined. Despite the fact that youth deaths have fallen since the 1990's, they are still many times higher than in comparable nations around the globe, yet the gun lobby accepts the situation. Children in the US are 67 times more likely to die by gun than children in the United Kingdom and 13 times more likely than in France[192].

There is no acceptable reason that the death rate among this nations' youth cannot be reduced to levels found in other industrialized nations. The only obstacle remains the arms industry and conservative Congressional ties to that industry. Manufacturers of firearms have done nothing to mitigate the death toll among children or adolescents, and lobbied ferociously for increasingly lenient regulations on firearms, at great cost to the nations' children.

Congress Refuses to Act

The refusal of Congress to put in place common sense systems to report on violent death and injury and a system for tracing firearms used in crime places the youth of our nation in jeopardy. Without studying the impact of firearms in the home, we cannot know the impact on youth and how we can mitigate the problem. It is on the insistence of the gun lobby that there is no realistic mechanism to study this problem.

The Peril for Women

The Multiple Threats to Women

Living in a home with firearms poses inordinate risks for women. Mothers who experience gun violence are twice as likely to experience anxiety and depression, as are women who do not experience violence in their communities[193]. Women living in communities with gun violence report poor health and sleep habits, risky behavior such as smoking, sexual adventurism and poor driving habits[194]. This in turn has an impact on the woman's ability to provide adequate care for her offspring, which has an impact on the child's social and emotional development.

The Heightened Risk of Death or Injury

The risk of death by firearm is high for American women, who have an increased risk of being killed by a spouse, lover or close relative with a record of domestic abuse[195]. For battered women, a fatal assault was 2.7 times more likely in those homes with firearms. There was no evidence of a defensive or preventative effect for women if guns were present in the home[196]. Homes with firearms were not safer, nor did the presence of firearms deter more crime than those without firearms. The presence of firearms in the home correlates with a risk of homicide three times that of homes without firearms. That risk increases to eight times if the offender is a partner or relative of the victim, and to twenty times where prior incidents of domestic violence exist[197].

The Hazard Posed by Intimate Partners

When guns are present in the home during domestic violence incidents, women are 12 times more likely to die than in homes without firearms[198]. When women are killed in the home, it is most likely to be her partner or a male relative with a record of domestic abuse, who is the killer[199]. In the U.S., two-thirds of women killed by their husbands are shot. Three times as many women are murdered by guns used by intimate partners, than are killed by strangers armed with guns, knives or other weapons combined[200].

In 1998, for every instance of fatal self-defense by a woman against an intimate acquaintance, 83 women were killed by an intimate acquaintance with a handgun[201]. In 2010, there were 1,800 homicides of women by men, and of those, 56.5% were intimate acquaintances of the killers[202]. In a study embracing 25 industrialized countries, the U.S. represents just 32% of the female population, but 84% of all female firearm homicides[203].

In the same year, for each incident in which a woman killed a stranger in self-defense, 497 women were murdered with a handgun, of which 260 were wives and 180 girlfriends. Overall, 101 women were murdered for each instance in which they killed in self-defense.

In 2005, 57.4% of the 1181 women killed by a boyfriend, spouse or ex-spouse were killed with firearms[204]. Children are also at increased risk of being killed in incidents of domestic violence. Perpetrators of intimate partner violence (IPV) are also more likely to use firearms to threaten and intimidate partners[205]. These threats by intimate partners are strong predictors of future homicides[206].

One survey comparing the gun possession practices of 417 women in 67 California women's shelters, at least one third of the battered women had a firearm in the home[207]. In two thirds of these cases, the intimate partner threatened to shoot or kill the woman (71.4%) or shot at her (5.1%). Almost sixty-five percent of the women reported that their partner used the gun to scare, threaten or harm her. Firearms in the home of battered women are generally more common than in the general household. In cases in which women used a firearm in self-defense, a third also used the weapon aggressively against a partner. Almost eighty percent of battered women reported that having a gun in the home made them feel less safe.

The Fatal Consequences of Guns and Domestic Violence

Comprehensive background checks for all firearm sales would help women immensely, as long as all restraining orders were included. Many women feel that their reports of abuse are not taken seriously, especially when their abusers are allowed to continue using and purchasing firearms. Conviction for domestic violence often does not result in criminal convictions; even a temporary restraining order should mandate removal of firearms from abusive men. If reporting abuse does not result in sanctions, women will be discouraged from reporting these crimes and more women will continue to suffer from intimidation, coercion, assault and death from shootings.

Although the U.S. does make gun possession illegal for abusive partners or those convicted of misdemeanor domestic violence, criminal records are the responsibility of the states, and many states do not capture domestic violence convictions into the federal database[208]. This is because the federal government cannot compel states to provide information on Serious Mental Illness, violent crime and domestic offenders. Naturally, many states, mostly Southern states, do not provide these data, resulting in ineffective background checks.

Additionally, temporary restraining orders do not fall under the compliance requisite, neither do couples who only live together, those in current or previous dating relationship, or unmarried couples with children, all of which leaves gaping gaps and room for misuse of the system. All of this could be prevented if Congressional Republicans mandated reporting for all these groups and removed their putative right to firearms.

Blood Money: How Company's Profit from Domestic Violence

Some companies actually profit from domestic violence. One company, Zombie Industries produced a target resembling a bleeding woman. This dummy, named "The Ex" is wearing a tight white shirt with violet bra and produces fake blood when shot[209]. This company also produced a target resembling President Obama. Actions like this are indicative of the contempt with which some in the gun community treat both women, and life. Far from defending against violence, gun owners who consume these products are far more likely to perpetuate violence.

Insurance companies may restrict or deny access to health care coverage or life insurance based on cases of domestic violence[210]. Not only are women in homes with guns more likely to be targets of firearm abuse, assault, intimidation, injury and death, but also based on those conditions, they may not be able to secure medical insurance. Domestic violence now constitutes a "preexisting condition" that may hike insurance rates or limit coverage. This discrimination is found across the insurance industry, health, life, disability, property and casualty insurance, which includes homeowners, personal automobile, commercial property and automobile[211].

The Refusal to Protect Abused Women

The gun lobby continues to obstruct legislation that would protect women from abusive spouses by prohibiting abusers from possessing guns. Many legislators want the state to be able to expropriate firearms from gun owners who have protective orders filed against them. The gun lobby opposes all such efforts based on the presumptive right to bear arms. As a result, far too many men kill their partners, and often themselves.

In California where confiscation of firearms for those with full protection orders is mandated by state law, the major crimes unit of San Mateo County reported that they had not had a single domestic violence related homicide in three years[212]. The gun lobby has defeated legislation in most states aimed at the mandatory removal of firearms from domestic violence situations. Even in states such as Washington, which authorizes judges to order the surrender of firearms if there is a compelling "serious and imminent threat" to public health, judges seldom apply these rules. Yet, a study in California of women who have requested restraining orders find that most wanted firearms removed from their abusive partners[213].

The New York Times studied cases in Washington state, and found that in a number of instances, women were shot to death less than a month after issuance of protection orders[214]. This is despite the women requesting that firearms be removed from their abusers home and the fact that intimate partner homicide accounts for almost half the women killed each year.

The 1994 crime bill included a provision prohibiting those with full protective orders from purchasing or possessing firearms. The gun lobby objected vehemently to this provision, and Congress complied by excluding those under temporary restraining orders, arguing that they have not yet been able to contest the allegations before a court[215]. A study of domestic violence restraining orders found that intimate partner homicide dropped significantly (19%) after the introduction of these laws[216].

The gun lobby opposes all attempts to introduce protective order bills, even in the case of full protective orders, sending messages to their members who deluge their representatives with objections. The gun lobby's position is that[217],

> "Any crime serious enough to cause an individual to lose a fundamental
> constitutional right should be classified as a felony".

Individuals can only be charged with a felony once they have committed a crime. The idea behind a protection order is to keep the abuser away from the abused. If abusers are able to obtain firearms, it is far too easy to commit homicides, by which time it is too late for the victim. Like the bullies in a schoolyard, the gun lobby favors the bullies and the violent in society, rather than those who are vulnerable to victimization and have a right to protection. Yet again, they demonstrate a lack of empathy for those who are victimized in deference to those who victimize.

In states like Washington State, there have been a number of attempts to introduce firearm removal laws for protective orders, but each one has been defeated after strong opposition from the gun lobby. Brian Judy, NRA lobbyist testified that one particular measure "granted broad authority to strip firearms rights". It seems that those bent on violence have rights, but abused women have none. Abusive men have shown that they are a danger to their partners, yet they receive greater legal protection than their victims who go without. Thus, the gun lobby stands for the violent and the abusers in society and not with the vulnerable, and the abused.

The issuance of restraining orders often incites extreme and violent emotion in the subject of the order. Gun proponents claim that the cases have not been tried in court, which violates the rights of the abuser. Society should remove any firearms from the scene to preclude the opportunity for violence. It is too late to lament the inaction of the legislative branch after a homicide. Once the accused has had his day in court, given a favorable judgment, or the protection order is lifted, his guns can be returned. We do not allow an accused murderer to keep his firearm until trial, there is no reason to extend any courtesy to violent abusers.

The gun lobby claims that these bills amount to confiscation, since they may require owners to sell their firearms. Each bill contains provision for the surrender of firearms to authorities, not confiscation, and they can be returned if the order is lifted. Conservatives cannot honestly claim that confiscation is worse than the fate that awaits women at the hands of abusive and violent men.

Wisconsin is a state with firearm surrender laws for full protective orders, but in an attempt to strengthen these laws, victims groups pushed for the listing of all firearms and their surrender within forty-eight hours of the issuance of a protective order. The gun lobby argued that this violates the Fifth Amendment rights against self-incrimination by forcing the gun possessor to admit to a crime. The bill did not pass, and women are once more subject to the violent extremes of their abusers.

In state after state, bills preventing the object of protective orders from possessing or purchasing firearms have failed, through gun lobby intimidation and antagonism. Due to these efforts, women are at far greater risk of severe injury or death than they would otherwise have been.

Republicans like Senate Minority Leader Bill Cadman, claim that these bills are ripe for misuse and could be used for confiscation of personal private property[218]. Anyone who chooses to assault or abuse a partner has lost the right to possess firearms. That is true of many forms of property used in the commission of a crime; there should be no exception made for firearms. Property rights are not more important than the right to life, or the absolute right to live without fear of violent partners. The Colorado protective order bill did not receive a single Republican vote, indicating that Republicans would rather vote with assailants than with their victims. The arms industry has become a willing and integral part of the endemic cycle of violence that plagues women and their children.

If we compare the relative harm imposed on each side, it is clear where the law should lie. On the one side, we have the very good chance that an abused woman may end up dead or severely injured; on the other, we have the alleged abusers gun rights removed. Removing the right to possess firearms for a short period does no harm any more than losing a vehicle license for a year is a tragedy. The law should favor and protect those who have suffered the greater harm or potential harm.

As well as threatening women who file protective orders, abusive men often threaten to harm or kill any man with whom the woman has contact, placing not only her life, but also the lives of others at increased risk of injury or death. It is common for abusive men to threaten members of their victims' family, parents, siblings or children, friends and even pets, to vent their anger. Society has a right to expect protection from potentially violent men, and removing the weapons with the greatest potential for harm is the most sensible way to handle these situations.

Republican members of Congress produce arguments against protective orders, saying for instance,

> "There are so many ways they (abusers) can get around this.... If they intend violence, if they intend to continue they pattern of domestic violence they are not going to tell you where the guns are. Or they are going to find a baseball bat or a knife."

If just one abuser surrenders his firearms, and that saves one life, that sufficiently justifies the laws. At the very least, abusers will be unable to use their firearms, and they can be charged if in possession of firearms. These legislators demonstrate a fundamental misunderstanding of the role legislation plays in the lives of citizens. The implication is an anarchic society, in which laws are made by those with guns. It is still more difficult to kill someone without a firearm than it is with one.

There is also a compelling link between domestic violence and mass shootings, as asserted in a study by Mayors Against Illegal

Guns. Of the 93 mass shootings between 2009 and 2012, the killer murdered a spouse, intimate partner or family member in fifty-three incidents, while seventeen shooters had previous domestic violence charges[219]. That includes Adam Lanza the Newtown killer, who murdered his mother before initiating his massacre.

The Second Amendment has failed to provide an avenue enabling women to protect themselves. Gun possession has proven a greater threat to the lives of women than the absence of firearms, and a tool for exploitation, intimidation and violence by abusers. Abusive men are more likely to murder their partners, and the presence of a firearm significantly increases the fatality rate[220]. Allowing an abusive man to keep firearms is tantamount to a death sentence for many abused women. The gun lobby opposes all laws restricting firearms to violent men, despite two million gun sales to prohibited purchasers prevented by the National Instant Criminal Background Check System, with 700,000 prohibitions in the last decade[221].

While background checks ensure that people with qualifying restraining orders are prevented from buying firearms from authorized dealers, there are ways around that, allowing violent abusers to buy firearms without a background check. The federal background check is thus only partially effective in preventing domestic abusers from buying firearms. In those states that have closed the private sale loophole, the number of women killed with a firearm by an intimate partner is 38% lower than in comparable states[222].

The gun lobby invariably stands in the way of societies' safety in their blind lust for firearm rights. Legislators ought to be doing whatever is in their power to prevent violent and abusive men from attacking their victims. The Supreme Court has affirmed the federal ban on gun possession by domestic violence offenders, including misdemeanor offenses involving an attack on a spouse, ex-spouse, or other members of a household. Whether the gun lobby like it or not, violent offenders cannot possess firearms. What the nation needs now is to shut the gun show loophole to prevent all abusers from acquiring firearms.

The Stalking Loophole

Like the subjects of protection orders, stalkers are still able to purchase and possess firearms, despite the threat that they pose to potential victims, especially women. An estimated one in six women experience stalking in their lifetimes, which induces fear or the belief that people close to them might be harmed or killed. One study determined that stalkers use weapons to harm or to threaten their victims in one of every five cases[223]. There is no federal law prohibiting their purchasing and possessing firearms, despite the fact that stalking is a crime. Stalking often leads to an escalation of violence when the objects of their affections do not comply with their desires. Congress has yet to address this problem with appropriate legislation.

The Intimidating Firearm

Death or injury by firearm in the home is only one way in which women are victims of gun violence. Guns are more often used by abusive partners to threaten, degrade or intimidate women, resulting in emotional trauma and fear. These firearms are used far more often against the occupants of the home, particularly women, than they are against intruders or in self-defense. Firearms are also used by intimate partners as coercion during rapes and other forms of sexual assault. The firearms used in these incidents are legally purchased and used against occupants of the home.

American men shoulder much of the blame for the victimization of women by ignoring the role that firearms play in domestic violence and intimidation. Men are more likely to own firearms and to fight for greater access to those firearms. Men, especially white men are far more likely to vote for Republican candidates, especially those who support gun possession, which increases gun ownership and exacerbates gun violence and the victimization of women. Male complacency also contributes significantly to the ongoing assaults and deaths by firearm.

Women need to make it abundantly clear to the men in their lives that gun violence is unacceptable, as is having a firearm in the home.

They need to vote to ensure that Congress can pass comprehensive gun restrictions, which provide greater security, safer communities and give their children peace of mind.

For too much of human history women have had the impression that men have the right to use violence against them, and too many men and women still believe this. A study of 25 countries found that where firearms are more available, more women are killed. In the U.S., particularly where gun ownership is higher, more women are killed than in comparable countries. In Canada, between 1995 when gun laws were tightened, and 2003, the gun homicide rate for women dropped 40%. In Australia after the Port Arthur massacre in 1996, stricter gun laws were introduced and the homicide rate for women dropped 57%[224].

In South Africa, the founders of Gun Free South Africa have been the targets of vitriolic, mostly white male rage. The women in this organization are targeted, through personal insults, abusive phone calls, and on talk radio and in the press. Adele Kirsten, co-founder of GFSA identified sexual and gender identity and colonial white male identity as the core of the crisis. This says much about the violence inherent in the gun owning community and begs the question, whether men with a violent disposition should be allowed to own firearms.

Buying a Firearm Makes Women Less Safe

Women who purchase a firearm are 50% more likely to be killed than are women who have not bought firearms; of those 45% were killed by an intimate partner with a gun[225]. In comparison, an intimate partner killed 20% of women murdered with a gun. The gun lobby claims that convincing women to purchase firearms is a public service, whereas in fact, their tactics are used to market firearms to vulnerable populations generally unwilling to use firearms. This increases the risk of injury or death for those women.

Guns, Youths and the College Campus

The idea that women will be safer on college campuses by carrying weapons is questionable. There is a real danger that entirely innocent young men could be shot by women fearful for their lives. Allowing concealed carrying of weapons on college campuses would make them more dangerous for women in threatening situations. Men are more likely to be carrying firearms than women, and more likely to use them, placing everyone, men and women at greatly elevated risk. Given the dramatically higher death and injury rate for young men of college age, the carrying of firearms on campuses is likely to increase the rate of death among that population. This group already has higher rates of alcohol and other substance abuse, increasing the risk of violent altercations and subsequent injury and death.

The Response of Congress to Violence against Women

The peremptory refusal of the gun lobby and Congressional Republicans to enact sensible anti-gun-violence laws is a continuation of the escalating war on women and other vulnerable populations. Women are more likely to lead the demand for greater anti-gun-violence legislation than they are to fight for increasingly negligent gun laws. Most women want safer communities for their children, respect for woman's human rights and fewer firearms in their homes and communities.

Republican obstructionism in renewing the Violence against Women Act, which includes provisions against the possession of firearms by people with restraining orders against them, reinforces the perception that conservatives and their gun lobby allies have little sympathy with battered and abused women. While Democrats managed to pass aspects of VAWA in the Senate, both Senate and House Republicans balked at passing the Act. Domestic violence prevention ought to be simple to pass, but clearly not to Republicans who believe that the rights of the oppressor supersede those of the victim.

Given the deplorable Republican reaction to rape, epitomized by such political luminaries as U.S. Rep. Todd Akin who spoke of "legitimate rape", it is not surprising that conservatives refused to renew VAWA. It did eventually pass despite the fact that Senators like Orrin Hatch did not appreciate the inclusion of LGBT communities and Native Americans. These communities are as likely to be victims of gun violence as any other, and in some cases, more so, particularly Native American communities in which violence against women is significantly higher. There is no reason that we cannot afford them protection from assault.

The state has a fundamental obligation to protect its residents from violence, intimidation and coercion. By permitting the unrestricted possession of firearms, the U.S. government and too many of the state governments have ignored that responsibility and created the conditions necessary for men to perpetuate violence against women. The gun lobby, by arrogating the putative right to gun possession, collude with sympathetic legislators to ignore continued violence against women.

Gun Injury Is Part of Health Care

The gun lobby finds waiting periods inconvenient. You have only to ask my husband how inconvenient he finds his wheelchair from time to time **(Sarah Brady)**

Gun injury and death is probably the most avoidable public health crisis faced by the United States. Yet, it is also the most ignored.

The gun lobby attempts to convince us that the academic right to bear arms prevents us from dealing with the resulting gun violence as part of public health. Gun injury is a preventable cause of tens of thousands of deaths and injuries each year, which cannot be dismissed just because it does not suit the gun lobby. The right to life is more important than the right to any material possession or ideological position. We do not ignore AIDS as a disease because certain groups do not believe people should use condoms. Such a stance would be morally reprehensible and irresponsible, as is the stance that we should not treat gun deaths as a public health hazard.

Stifling the Health Care Debate

The President's desire to treat gun violence as a health care issue after Newtown outraged gun extremists, yet gun violence is about the public health. To the 100,000 people killed or injured in this country each year, their health is of paramount importance. Yet, intellectual luminaries like Rush Limbaugh, royal diva of talk radio, insist that firearm death and injury should not be treated as a health care issue. Doctors should be able to talk to their patients about the risks of gun ownership, just as they do about the risks of smoking, taking drugs or consuming a healthy diet. Doctors are there to warn us about the risks that our lifestyles pose to our lives, not to enrich pharmaceutical companies.

While gun massacres are isolated incidents that occur in one town or city, their impact is felt across the nation, and across the globe. After the theater shootings in Aurora, Colorado, cinemagoers in New York City were reluctant to attend showings because of the fear of another shooting. Anxiety, depression and panic attacks are common in the public after massacres, according to some mental health professionals[226].

Similarly, the shooting of Trayvon Martin, a seventeen-year old youth in Sanford, Florida induced fear in the community and made people worry about moving around at night. Concerns about how to react if assailed by a George Zimmerman style vigilante can overwhelm children and parents and lead to overly paranoid concerns for their own safety.

Post-traumatic stress resulting from a widely publicized massacre or shooting can weigh heavily on communities. In communities with high rates of gun violence, residents often exhibit higher levels of post-traumatic stress, exacerbated by the lack of medical care. The impact on vulnerable populations, such as children, adolescents and the mentally ill may be worse than for other groups.

Why should we not do everything we can to mitigate gun violence, and if that means a war on that violence, that is what we need to do. Conservatives appear to feel that we should do nothing to stem the violence, and in fact allow an ever-greater number of firearms on the street rather than tackle the problem. In this way, the gun lobby creates and aggravates the gun violence problem for society.

The National Epidemic of Gun Injury

Between 1950 and 2005, the death rate from all causes declined from 1,446 to 799 deaths per 100,000. This was partly due to our ability to deal with heart disease, stroke, and infant mortality. In contrast, the murder rate in 2005 was 20% higher than it was in 1950[227]. We take evidence-based solutions to disease prevention more seriously than we do for violence. We have little evidence about gun violence prevention, due to the intransigence and irrational fears of the gun lobby about government confiscating guns.

Excluding natural causes of deaths and considering only injury deaths, firearm deaths are second only to automobile accidents as the leading cause of death. The health care profession has successfully reduced natural deaths for many decades by focusing on the causes and implementing reduction strategies. Researchers in the CDC have been prevented by law from doing the same for firearm death. The gun lobby will not even consider the possibility of scientific studies into gun violence, or sensible steps to reduce that violence.

In the Culture of Violence Summit at Princeton University, the Princeton President Shirley M. Tilghman had this to say[228],

> "In the context of public health, an epidemic is what we face, the US has the most guns, the weakest gun laws and by far the highest rates of gun homicide, gun suicide and accidental gun death among developed nations."

As much as the gun lobby and conservative radio host Rush Limbaugh want it otherwise, any injuries or deaths are part of the public health debate. This country refuses to have this debate, because of an unwarranted fear of the gun lobby. When people die preventable deaths, we attempt to mitigate those deaths and injuries using whatever tools we have.

Tilghman continued that[229]

> "We have to deal with gun violence not in terms of the Second Amendment, but in terms of concrete national well-being, much as we have dealt with smoking in public settings, industrial emissions or the use of seatbelts."

Steven Altschuler, CEO of the Children's Hospital of Philadelphia, pointed out the success of the automobile industry, which used experts in

> "Epidemiology, biomechanics, engineering and behavioral science working in tandem to contribute to a dramatic decline in the numbers of children injured in car crashes".

The National Physicians Alliance views gun violence as a public health issue. Their policy recommendations include[230]

> "Stronger regulation of firearms, funding for research on gun violence, federal protection for clinical free speech and improved access to and support of mental health services".

Creating Gun Violence by Taking Away Health Services

The lack of access to the mental health system can also exacerbate the problem of gun violence. Forty to 45 million people in the US now have untreated depression. Of the 21% of children aged 9 to 17 who have mental illness or substance abuse issues in Minnesota, only

1 in 5 receives treatment[231]. While mental illness alone does not appear to have any direct impact on gun violence, suicide may be problematic for those with these diseases. Limiting access to firearms, especially for those with mental illness may help mitigate suicide.

Overemphasizing Mental Health in Massacres

Policy makers should also be careful that policy prescriptions do not overplay the importance of mental illness in gun deaths. Attributing deaths during gun massacres to mental illness only serves to stigmatize and marginalize people who suffer from mental illness with little compelling evidence that Severe Mental Illness leads to violence. People suffering from mental illness are more likely to be the victims of gun violence than its perpetrator[232]. While many perpetrators of high profile crimes may have experienced mental illness, there is little compelling evidence that mental illness caused the violent act. It may have exacerbated it, but it may well be that some other singular trigger precipitated the event. That illuminates at least one reason that we need to study gun violence, to learn how to prevent violent acts before they occur.

To successfully reduce gun violence through health care, we need to study potentially aggravating factors that may have more impact than mental health, including substance abuse, poverty, a record of violent abuse, social isolation and most importantly, access to firearms. Mental illness in concert with one or more of those factors may lead to gun violence, but without studying these issues and implementing public policy solutions that address the problem holistically, gun violence is unlikely to change. The characteristics of gun violence, prevention or reduction of gun related injuries; technologies to reduce gun violence and possible impact of video games, and traditional and social media all urgently need to be researched[233].

Children Using Guns to Commit Suicide

The routine deaths and injuries of children through suicide or accidental death is also a public health issue that ought to be tackled by legislators. These injuries and deaths happen because of firearm availability in the home or communities. In a study in the Denver area using data between the two shootings in Columbine and the Aurora theater, the injuries sustained by children were far more likely to lead to death than other traumatic injuries, with 50.4% requiring intensive care compared with 19.3% for other trauma related injury[234].

A Vast Conspiracy by Government to Co-opt Doctors

Many conservatives insist that doctors are required to pressure patients concerning gun use. Lou Dobbs rails against Obama transforming doctors into "agents of the federal government"[235]. Doctors are now seen by conservatives as having been recruited into the war on gun violence. Yet, the emergency system in this nation has to tackle the unceasing trauma related directly to gun possession, the 106 deaths by firearm and the more than 220 firearm injuries each day. This is a health care disaster and it is costing taxpayers dearly. Many doctors, especially trauma surgeons, are forced to encounter gun violence each day, and have an obligation to ensure that society is doing whatever it can to mitigate death and injuries.

The American firearm lifestyle poses a far greater risk to life than the lifestyle of other developed nations. Doctors need to communicate this to their patients. Many people would prefer that their physicians not paper over the cracks in our society; I want the truth as the facts inform us, not as the extreme right-wing fringe wants it to be. If doctors need to inform their patients about something that may save their lives, patients have a right to know. Economist Ted Miller stated to Bloomberg News, *"Gun ownership is like smoking, an expensive and dangerous habit"*[236].

Gun Control is Ineffective, Disease Kills More People

The skeptics of a health care approach to gun violence dispense much false information in order to disparage medical professionals. They attempt to show that other health issues kill more people than firearms, which is to misunderstand the reasons for treating this as a health care issue. To say that heart disease kills more people than guns and that we should concentrate on that aspect of health care misses the point. Guns are the proximate cause of unnecessary and preventable violent death that other developed nations do not experience to the same degree as in the U.S. Heart disease or cancer is treated as a public health issue that affects a great many people; similarly, we should treat gun violence as a preventable cause of death. We do not ignore one cause of death because another causes a greater number of deaths.

The presence of firearms turns everyday violence into fatalities. If a firearm is used during a domestic violence incident, there is a 23-fold increase in the likelihood of death[237]. From a public health perspective, if we know of a pathogen that causes a given disease, in this case gun violence, we do whatever we can to neutralize that pathogen.

Gun Violence Disproportionately Affects the Poor

To effectively reduce gun violence especially in poverty-ridden inner cities, the question of changing the socio-economic imbalance in society must be treated effectively. It is only when youths and their communities believe that they have a reasonable chance of success that they can abandon a culture of violence. When youths feel that there is no hope of improving economic opportunities in society, the inevitable result is social isolation and a turn to violence. The reluctance of Republican lawmakers in most states to tackle unemployment with public infrastructure spending and education is a major underlying cause of escalating violence. The ubiquity of firearms only provides disaffected youths and others with the convenient instrument of death and injury. The large sums of money a society uses to treat firearm injuries could easily be diverted into poverty alleviation programs.

Dorothy Stoneman founder of YouthBuild USA found that when youths are lifted out of poverty, they readily abandon the culture of violence and demonstrate a readiness to embrace a productive lifestyle[238].

Gun Violence is Not a Criminal Justice Issue

Opponents of the public health approach believe that gun violence is a criminal justice problem and worry that research into firearms by health organizations may result in campaigns to ban firearms[239]. Health professionals want to reduce the death and injuries caused by firearms through prevention before they occur, since they treat gunshot wounds on a regular basis. Once a patient comes into an emergency room with a gunshot wound, it is too late. While there may be a compelling social need to ban certain firearms, especially those that do the most harm, or are used in the majority of shootings, there is no medical agenda to take all guns away.

Using the criminal justice system to treat gun violence does nothing to reduce gun deaths and injuries, and only postpones a rational process for ending that violence. Society cannot afford to react to gun violence after that violence occurs. No society can flourish using reactive rather than proactive approaches to resolve problems.

We have tried the criminal justice approach, and we now incarcerate a greater proportion of our population than any other developed nation. This has not helped to alleviate violence and especially gun violence. We still have similar rates of violent crimes to other developed nations, and in most cases, more so.

Cooperation Will Reduce Gun Violence

The gun lobby steadfastly refuses to cooperate with society to reduce gun violence. Sensible limitations on firearms and accessories would go a long way towards achieving this goal.

A doctor in Lima, Ohio, concerned at the number of African-Americans in his office suffering from bullet wounds, turned to hip-hop to help alleviate the problem. He wrote down lyrics with a message about gun violence; artists refined those lyrics into rap to make them appeal to a young audience[240]. The doctor hands CD's to his patients to help spread the word.

If society can cooperate in solving or at least mitigating death and illness by cancer, AIDS, malaria, TB, high rates of vehicle accidents, drug abuse and smoking, surely it is possible for all sides of the gun debate to cooperate in reducing gun violence. The gun lobby refuses to even debate the reasons for gun violence and the means to end it. Their answer to every approach, scientific or otherwise is to demand more access to guns, more dangerous weapons, more deadly ammunition, and ever more parts of the country in which they can carry their destructive devices, with a total disregard for the wishes of non gun owners.

Public policy changes to prevent unintentional poisoning focused on limiting access to properly vetted users, reductions in toxicity, education and counseling. This approach reduced childhood death from poisoning by 75% over 20-years[241].

Similarly, the implementation of regulations governing driver education, licensing, speed limits, seat belt and child seats, and drunk driving, as well as modifications to vehicles such as safety glass, collapsible steering columns, padded interiors, seat belts and air bags assisted in reducing the death rate per mile by more than 90%[242]. Restricting gun possession to those with training or licensing, and modifications to the physical attributes of firearms to reduce lethality, improve child-proofing, limitations on ammunition strength, firearm caliber and so on may reduce the incidence of death and injury.

This public health argument is reminiscent of a debate in South Africa about AIDS. When it was suggested that men use condoms to prevent or reduce AIDS, black men claimed that it was a white conspiracy to prevent them from having children[243]. The net result was that AIDS deaths kept spiraling upwards. It is similar with firearms; gun owners do not see that they can use firearms responsibly, but use restrictions to reduce gun violence, death and injury. In neither case the condoms nor the guns, was there a plot to take guns or reproductive rights away; the intent with gun regulation is to reduce access to those firearms that cause the worst injuries or the most common injuries, and save life.

All Privileges and Rights Should Have Boundaries

Giving unregistered guns to untrained, unlicensed residents without any restrictions whatsoever is like giving a bicycle to a child without instructions. A responsible parent will instruct the child that he should not take the bicycle onto the street, and if he does, the parent should take the bicycle away. When the child is able to ride more skillfully, he may be allowed short trips under supervision. At all times the child should wear protective gear, such as helmets or gloves, or knee pads. If parents do not insist on these things, they are being irresponsible.

When children refuse to adhere to these rules and to the rules of the road, their privileges should be revoked. It is the same with firearms; too many owners are irresponsible, this is why we need rules, to inform them of the boundaries to that privilege. When they show that they are irresponsible, and behave like petulant children by insisting on assault weapons, silencers, armor piercing bullets or large quantities of ammunition, their privileges should be revoked. Other members of society, whether it be road users, or just residents have the right to be safe from irresponsible road users or equally irresponsible gun owners.

Some public health advocates believe that we cannot simply see gun violence in terms of gun regulation, but that we need a multidisciplinary approach to the problem, using the expertise and proven methods of a wide variety of people to mitigate gun violence[244]. To my mind, this is what gun restrictions entail, attacking the problem from a number of directions, the most important of which is controlling the source of the problem, which is the availability of firearms.

Gun Ownership Should Be Seen as Socially Unacceptable Behavior

The fundamental approach for public health policies is to change societal norms, and to make certain destructive behavior socially unacceptable. This was an accepted approach to cigarette smoking, the unregulated use of illicit and prescription drugs, public drunkenness including driving while intoxicated, and unprotected sex. These campaigns were largely successful at reducing the risks to life.

The prevalence of cigarette smoking was reduced from 43% to 19% between 1966 and 2010[245], for instance by using tobacco taxes to fund prevention. A similar approach needs to be taken with firearms. A tax on firearm and ammunition sales could fund prevention efforts. This tax could be used to compensate the victims of gun violence or their families, or to enforce existing laws. Possession of firearms ought to be seen as a threat to society, given the unacceptably high number of deaths and injuries each year. The true costs of firearm deaths and injuries to society are not reflected in the current sales taxes on firearms and related equipment[246].

Society has a right to expect gun owners to pay the costs of their habit, as society is increasingly implementing with cigarette smoking. Punitive taxes should be levied on firearms, ammunitions and accessories to help defray the costs incurred by gun violence. The rest of society should not have to bear the burden of their behavior, or to subsidize gun violence.

The Firearm Idol

Another approach might be to stop venerating firearms, or seeing them as enhancing masculinity or power. Firearms should be seen for what they are, destructive weapons that serve little social purpose other than to take life, cause grave injury and exact an economic toll on society. Society should begin to equate firearms with cowardice, weakness and aberrant or deviant behavior rather than as somehow heroic as portrayed in popular culture[247]. Similar approaches have been used successfully with cigarettes, drugs and alcohol.

What Gun Violence Costs Taxpayers

Considering the enormous public cost of gun violence, by various estimates between $60 Billion and $100 Billion each year and the cost in lives lost, this is one of the most important public health issues extant today. We as a nation spend vast amounts on combating the flu each year, on smoking reduction programs, or E. coli in foods, and yet we balk at tackling the root causes of gun violence. It is as though those lives placed in jeopardy by contaminated foods are vastly more important than those lost to gun violence. If studies find that gun restriction is likely to reduce gun deaths, it is our moral duty to enforce gun regulation, regardless of any alleged constitutional impediments.

Suffocating Research into Gun Violence

In the wake of massacres like Newtown and Aurora, there was little information to be gleaned from the nations premiere health care agency, the Centers for Disease Control. Since federal statute prohibits the agency from studying gun violence, it maintains no information that might serve to explain gun violence, or public policy prescriptions for the prevention of gun violence. Government is there in part to provide information not available in the private sphere, to ensure the safety of its residents and to explain the steps to take in the wake of tragedies.

At one time, public health agencies produced valuable statistics concerning gun violence and its resolution. The gun lobby, along with a submissive Congress passed an appropriations bill banning government funding for research used to promote gun regulation. This forced the Centers for Disease Control out of the research business[248]. The CDC is tasked with protecting people from unnecessary death and injury by whatever cause, including gun injury and death. It is irrational that they can study automobile accidents, communicable disease and cancers, but gun violence is excluded from their remit, purely because of the erroneous interpretation of the Second Amendment and political lobbyists. To his credit, President Obama issued an executive order on January 16, 2013, allowing the CDC to proceed with research into gun violence.

Research involved with the causes of gun violence is essential to resolving the underlying causes of gun violence. Without knowing what the causes are, we cannot begin to tackle the social effects of gun violence. The research and its recommendations and results are politically neutral, and can be used by all sides in the gun debate.

Research is done not to favor a political ideology, but to determine the root causes of any public health issue or danger to the state or its citizens.

Since conservatives, especially Republicans, introduced amendments preventing the collection of gun violence data by the CDC, they must take responsibility for the inability of citizens to cope in the wake of tragedies.

It is questionable whether firearms can ever be considered a safe product, given the *prima facie* reasons for firearm ownership; self-defense, which costs human lives; hunting, which destroys endangered wildlife; and environmental degradation caused by the lead in bullets. Add to that the homicides, life-threatening or life-altering injury, accidental death, intimidation, fear, the economic impoverishment of poorer communities due to gun violence and the export of small arms to strife-torn parts of the world, and firearms have no place in a civilized, peaceful society.

With the worrying recent increases in death and injury by firearm, while other forms of death, such as automobile accidents are falling, the need to study this issue is more compelling than ever. There are no decent data available on the number of firearms in the country. Some data collected by the ATF are not available to researchers, and data collected by the National Violent Death Reporting System from police departments and Medical Examiner offices only obtain data from a third of states[249]. Without these data, it is difficult to answer questions about gun violence or determine whether programs are working.

The gun lobby refuses to countenance the collection of gun statistics from fear of a national registry. Yet, there is no need to create a registry in order to promote public health. Personally identifying data can be stripped out of data, allowing researchers to study gun ownership and its relationship to violence unimpeded by personal data. Since researchers work with aggregates, averages or subsets of data, individually identifying data is not necessary. It is only because the gun lobby is afraid of the results that they fight so hard against it. If it indeed shows that guns are responsible for tens of thousands of deaths, which I have no doubt they are, their primary arguments in favor of gun ownership will fail.

It is a national disgrace that we have a great deal of data concerning every cause of death other than firearms merely because gun extremists are neurotic about having their guns confiscated. Reducing lives lost to gun violence has nothing to do with the Second Amendment. There is a great deal of blood on the hands of those in the gun lobby who obstruct the collection of these data. The sanctity of the living must always be our paramount concern.

The Intolerance of Targeting the Mentally Ill

The suggestion that mental illness is at the root of the nations' gun violence is highly contentious. Many millions of people suffer some form of mental illness during their lives, and commit few crimes. The percentage of people with mental illness who commit crimes are likely to be comparable to the proportion of the general population who commit crimes. Aggravating circumstances like divorce, unemployment or other stressful situation or drugs or alcohol abuse may play a more significant role in acts of violence. Mental illness alone, even severe mental illness appears to have little correlation with acts of violence.

Mental illness implies muddled or confused thinking, an inability to plan or organize, including routine tasks such as personal grooming, healthcare, shopping, or dressing. The ability to leave the home and socialize is often also impaired. Mental illness disrupts a persons thinking, mood, routine functioning or ability to relate to others. These medical conditions reduce the ability to cope with ordinary life. This may result in increased risk to members of the household, but are less likely to spill over to the community. People with mental illness are less likely to socialize or take part in community activities, with many preferring seclusion.

Only a very small percentage of those with mental health issues commit crimes. At a Janus Forum event, "Guns in America", Richard Friedman, Cornell University professor of clinical psychiatry maintained that only about four percent of gun deaths can be attributed to those with mental illness[250]. Yet, people in responsible positions want to regulate those with mental health issues, but not those who own guns. The gun lobby claims that only a small number of gun owners commit gun crimes, but the same can be said of those with mental illness. Perhaps we should test gun owners for paranoia and delusion before they are allowed to own guns.

Estimates put the number of people with diagnosable mental health issues at 26.2% of the population over 18 years of age in any given year[251]. By that measure, much of the population may be prohibited from owning a firearm. A more restrictive measure might be Major Depressive Disorders, or 6.7% of the population, bipolar at 2.6% or schizophrenia at 1.1% of the population. Someone needs to determine which people with mental illness are likely to become violent, or to commit suicide; perhaps it would be simpler to put everyone with a mental illness in the same pigeonhole.

A Maryland state task force found that only those with Severe Mental Illness have an elevated risk of committing shooting sprees, and only when aggravated by drugs or alcohol. Even the Severely Mentally Ill only commit crimes at a level slightly elevated from the general population. There appears to be little evidence that people with other mental problems commit crimes with any greater frequency than the public.

Stigmatizing the Mentally Ill

The targeting and stigmatizing of those with varying degrees of mental illness, from depression to the most serious schizophrenia or bipolar disorder, is a hallmark of tyrannical regimes the world over. In lieu of finding real solutions to societal problems, it is always easier to blame vulnerable groups like the mentally ill for those problems. This further marginalizes those with mental illness by claiming that all of society's depravities can be laid at their door, and that we need look no further for a cause. It is easy to mark those who appear radically different from the great mass of humanity, and to invoke the specter of danger where none exists.

The New York State legislature requires mental health professionals to report any patient at risk of harming themselves or others. Mental health professionals fear that the system will be riddled with false positives, and discourage the mentally ill from seeking help[252]. Targeting the mentally ill only violates basic human rights while doing nothing to address the root causes of gun violence.

Adam Lanza reportedly had Aspberger's, a syndrome that prevents sufferers from participating successfully in social interactions. Whether that is true is debatable, but it does not answer the question of what ultimately caused Lanza to kill so many. It is unlikely that a person with mental illness is able to think coherently, or methodically plan and execute a complex plan to slaughter children. It is more likely that Lanza just lacked empathy towards his targets.

Instead of tackling the admittedly difficult task of ridding society of firearms, society fiddles around the edges of the problem, using solutions that have no reasonable chance of success, and are unlikely to be implemented. Providing access to mental health services is a laudable goal, but is unlikely to stop gun massacres. Placing people on a mental health database, regardless of the threat they may pose to society, or forcing patients into treatment programs, then surveilling, restricting and stigmatizing those people is a governmental affront to power far worse than tracking gun owners. Actions of this type convince the public that people with mental health issues are a danger to society, which further stigmatizes them and does little to curb gun violence.

Overwhelmingly, people who appear, at least outwardly, to be normal, carry out gun violence and homicides. Natural human aggression is more likely to blame than mental illness, and the unrestricted access to extreme weaponry is more likely to make any instance of violence lethal than is mental illness.

Wayne LaPierre, NRA chief had this to say,

> "The truth is that our society is populated by an unknown number of genuine monsters."

We should question whether those monsters include those who force extreme weapons on a vulnerable society, and then blame others for the resulting disasters. Many nations have a similar population mix to our own, which would include "monsters", and yet gun massacres and gun crimes do not happen in those nations to the extent that they do here. If the sole distinction between those nations and the U.S. is too many firearms, too many firearm deaths and too many gun lobbyists, perhaps those promoting firearms are the true monsters. A nation that experiences large numbers of gun crimes, homicides and injuries and does nothing but demand more guns is experiencing collective insanity. Despite the overwhelming evidence that gun regulations work, the demand for access to increasingly extreme weapons continues unabated, which appears anything but sane.

It is likely that mass killers are motivated not by mental illness or psychiatric disorder, but by extreme anger or resentment at some segment of society. Given the relative paucity of evidence implicating mental illness, perhaps gun owners should be tested for anger management issues and denied gun access based on the results.

The Mentally Ill Are the Victims of Crime

People with mental health issues are more likely to be victims of crime than perpetrators. One analysis found that "*25% of people with mental illness are likely to be victims of violence as compared to 3% of the general population*"[253]. Studies show that those with severe mental illness are more likely to pose a danger to themselves than to others. People with mental health issues are far more likely to kill themselves than harm others.

Swedish researchers found that people with mental illness are five times more likely to be murdered than are people without mental illness, and if they take drugs, nine times more likely to be murdered[254]. The public is a greater threat to patients with mental illness than those with mental illness are to the public.

If 26.2% of the population has a diagnosable mental illness, but those with mental illness only commit an estimated 3-5% of gun crimes, logic suggests that people with these diseases are less likely than the general population to commit violent acts with firearms. Yet, 38 states irrationally maintain a registry of the mentally ill for use in background checks[255].

Targeting the mentally ill after gun massacres is not only misplaced, but also biased and misinformed. People displaying common human aggression using easily obtained firearms carry out most homicides. The mentally ill are just being used as a convenient target for gun lobbyists who refuse to accept the necessity of registering gun owners. Adding insult to injury, the Gun Control Act of 1968 refers to individuals who have been committed to a mental institution as "mental defectives"[256].

Mistaken Assumptions about Mass Shooting and Mental Illness

Members of the public, encouraged by the gun lobby and too many in the media echo chamber automatically assume that the perpetrators of mass shootings are mentally ill. However, there is a paucity of evidence suggesting that perpetrators are mentally ill. Even in those cases in which there is some history of mental illness, it is unclear what part mental illness plays in most massacres, if any. While some researchers find that perpetrators are deeply troubled people, they do not seem to exhibit symptoms of psychosis and few have a "history of contact with mental health services"[257].

In a New York Times post, Joe Nocera says[258],

> "Anyone who goes into a school with a semi-automatic and kills 20 children and six adults is by definition mentally ill."

While the massacre may be heinous, it is feasible that the killer was lucid, but was livid over some perceived sleight, was recalling some act of bullying, or had an argument with a parent, sibling or peer. It is as likely that he took out his anger at society by perpetrating the massacre as that he was seriously mentally ill, or if he was, that his illness precipitated the killings. It is as likely that shooters are motivated by revenge, jealousy, abuse, peer intimidation or lack of respect. Society cannot judge the mental state of someone without examining that person, or at the very least examining his medical records. Even then, that does not necessarily imply motive. In the Rwandan genocide, half a million people were slaughtered, but it is unlikely that the killers were all insane; it is as likely that they were apathetic to their depravities, or deluded or angry.

Mass shootings require planning, organization, preparation and the ability to obtain and use firearms. The symptoms of serious mental illness such as schizophrenia include disordered and muddled thinking, which are not conducive to the actions required to commit mass murder. Attributes common among mass killers are social isolation, lack of social skills, introversion and sometimes paranoia. None of those conditions necessarily suggests an increased tendency to violence[259].

Dramatically Increased Public Expenditure on Mental Illness Rather Than Gun Restrictions

Conservatives are quick to blame mental illness for massacres, while showing little sympathy for the mentally ill when it comes to social expenditure on health care. Yet, with the gun lobby's refusal to countenance background checks for anyone purchasing a gun, they are implicitly affirming the right of those with criminal records, records of Severe Mental Illness and others to purchase assault style weapons, or any hand gun without exception.

The gun lobby are implicitly accepting that anyone, regardless of their condition or threat to society, be extended the right to purchase firearms. They lobby furiously to allow anyone to purchase weapons, and Congress, state houses and governors accept and embrace this view.

For mental illness screening to be effective, 300 million Americans would require testing for mentally illness. Screeners must determine whether any particular individual is likely to be a threat with a firearm. The screening of 60 million gun owners is a gargantuan task. Since the mentally ill contribute so little to overall violence, prohibiting those with mental illness from gun possession is unlikely to have a significant impact on routine gun violence. However, it may reduce suicides.

There is no way to predict, other than capricious precognition, whether a person is likely to pose a significant danger to society. It is far more sensible to restrict access to extreme firearms and ammunition, and prevent known felons, domestic abusers, stalkers and others from any firearm ownership. The executive actions of President Obama relating to mental health issues are unlikely to have any impact on gun violence. Additionally, the gun lobby is far more likely to oppose government spending on mental health issues than to favor spending. Funding for research into gun violence and improving mental health services is unlikely given gun lobby opposition and Conservative insistence on budget control.

A bill in Congress introduced by Sen. Mark Pryor would actually make it easier for those with mental illness to purchase firearms. People released from a psychiatric hospital, even if placed there involuntarily can demand that their names be removed from the NICS database used for background checks[260].

Should We Register The Mentally Ill, or Gun Owners?

In the wake of Newtown, the NRA hypocritically demanded a national registry for persons with mental illness, while opposing a gun registry. Guns are significantly more dangerous to society than people with mental illness. According to databases that track gun homicides, only 3-5% of gun crimes involve mentally ill shooters, which is a lower incidence than the general population[261].

Given this fact and the danger of firearms, the NRA should demand a national registry for firearms and their owners. Mass shootings happen too infrequently to make generalized statements about mental illness. Murders by people with psychosis occur at roughly one per 14 million in other nations, whereas stranger homicide in the U.S. occurs at around 140 per 14 million. A registry of gun owners makes far more sense than one for the mentally ill.

Substance Abuse, Not Mental Illness Needs a Registry

Alcohol abuse or dependence is more likely to be related to violent and impulsive crime, than mental illness alone[262]. Instead of targeting those with mental illness, we should concentrate on those with substance abuse issues, who are more likely to commit crime, and prohibit people with addiction from owning firearms. Gender, geographic region and race are all better predictors of gun violence than mental illness[263]. Instead of a registry for people with mental illness, registration of Southern males with substance abuse issues may go further towards mitigating gun violence.

Some mental disorders are correlated with a lower risk of violence compared to the general population. There is little data to suggest that mental health interventions reduce violence. Even if science were able to correctly diagnose those with a propensity to commit violence, there is little to suggest that current treatments would effectively prevent them from committing acts of violence.

Mass Killers and Psychopathy

It is somewhat feasible that mass killers like Adam Lanza are psychopathic or sociopathic, or at least exhibit some of the symptoms of those classifications. However, psychopathy is not a defined mental disorder, or certainly not one sanctioned by the mental health profession. Strictly speaking, it is not a malfunction in the brain. It may instead manifest as lack of conscience, guilt, empathy or remorse, narcissism, pathological lying, superficial charm, shallow emotions, or inability to accept responsibility[264].

There does not appear to be a cure for these traits, although the British government is trying to define Dangerous and Severe Personality Disorder[265] as a legal classification. We should determine how many gun owners satisfy the general criteria of psychopathy. As a society, we should be able to test for this predisposition to prevent gun violence. A great many people may exhibit some of these personality traits, but never commit acts of violence. A propensity to commit violent acts is not necessarily in and of itself a diagnosable condition.

Ready access to lethal weapons may make it easier for some people with these tendencies to perpetrate violent acts and to take a great many lives. A lack of empathy may make it more difficult for them to fully comprehend the ramifications of their actions.

Conclusion

We should stop blaming the mentally ill for society's inability to control firearms. The burden of gun violence and gun massacres should be placed on the shoulders of the gun industry, the gun lobby and ultimately gun owners, not on those who are unable to fight back. It is always easy to target the vulnerable.

Conclusion

The case for gun restrictions, considering the evidence is compelling. Sensible nations have shown that it is possible to introduce successful. Those nations show that restrictions reduce gun deaths and injuries. Even the most restrictive nations still allow some gun ownership, and manage black markets.

Victims, non-gun-owners and society have the right to determine which steps will keep communities safe. Prohibiting threats to local and national security, like the assault weapon, is an essential action to take. Responsible gun owners should embrace such steps.

We need to understand that there is an unacceptable level of risk in firearm ownership, and that there are ways to resolve conflict other than taking life.

The flow of guns to troubled elements in society is exacerbated by the ease with which people obtain firearms. Straw purchases, gun shows, background-check free trading all increase gun trafficking and gun crime.

The death toll in America is unacceptably high, and we do little to prevent it rising. The cost of gun restrictions is minimal and there are few benefits to gun ownership, while the costs of gun ownership are a burden on victims, their families and friends, and on society.

Even children are not immune, with increased access to guns through parents, peers and society. The gun industry entices children in much the same way as drug dealers, which encourages gun accidents, suicides and homicides.

Women are just as vulnerable to gun violence through intimate partners, stalkers and relatives, as are those with mental illness. The firearm is a powerful tool used for intimidation, assault, injury and homicide.

We need to see firearms as a threat to health, not merely as a criminal justice issue. We can succeed in the battle against gun violence.

Keep an eye out for my next books; *"Gun Sanity"* and *"Unacceptable Losses"*.

Notes

[1] The data from this invaluable website is accessible at <http://www.gunpolicy.org/>

[2] <http://www.motherjones.com/> . A general news website. Their data on mass shootings was invaluable.

[3] < http://www.cdc.gov/injury/wisqars/fatal_injury_reports.html>. Centers for Disease Control. Accessed November 16th, 2013.

[4] <http://papers.ssrn.com/sol3/papers.cfm?abstract_id=1030802> . "Can handguns be effectively regulated." June 2nd, 2013.James Jacobs New York University School of Law. David Kairys Temple University - Beasley Schools of Law. University of Pennsylvania Law Review PENNumbra, Vol. 156, p. 188, 2007.

[5] <http://papers.ssrn.com/sol3/papers.cfm?abstract_id=1030802> . "Can handguns be effectively regulated." June 2nd, 2013.James Jacobs New York University School of Law. David Kairys Temple University - Beasley Schools of Law. University of Pennsylvania Law Review PENNumbra, Vol. 156, p. 188, 2007.

[6] <http://papers.ssrn.com/sol3/papers.cfm?abstract_id=1030802> . "Can handguns be effectively regulated." June 2nd, 2013.James Jacobs New York University School of Law. David Kairys Temple University - Beasley Schools of Law. University of Pennsylvania Law Review PENNumbra, Vol. 156, p. 188, 2007.

[7] <http://papers.ssrn.com/sol3/papers.cfm?abstract_id=1030802> . "Can handguns be effectively regulated." June 2nd, 2013.James Jacobs New York University School of Law. David Kairys Temple University - Beasley Schools of Law. University of Pennsylvania Law Review PENNumbra, Vol. 156, p. 188, 2007.

[8] <http://papers.ssrn.com/sol3/papers.cfm?abstract_id=1030802> . "Can handguns be effectively regulated." June 2nd, 2013.James Jacobs New York University School of Law. David Kairys Temple University - Beasley Schools of Law. University of Pennsylvania Law Review PENNumbra, Vol. 156, p. 188, 2007.

9 Japan. 2001. 'Firearms Control in Japan.' National Police Agency, Firearms Division, p. 6. Tokyo: Firearms Division, Community Safety Bureau, National Police Agency. 1 January.

[10] <http://finance.yahoo.com/news/gun-control-advocates-scored-major-180559145.html> . Walter Hickey. "Gun Control Advocates have scored a major victory that nobody is talking about." April 16th, 2013.

[11] <http://en.wikipedia.org/wiki/District_of_Columbia_v._Heller>. *District of Culumbia v. Heller*. 554 U.S. 570 (2008).

[12] <http://papers.ssrn.com/sol3/papers.cfm?abstract_id=1030802> . "Can handguns be effectively regulated." June 2nd, 2013.James Jacobs New York University School of Law. David Kairys Temple University - Beasley Schools of Law. University of Pennsylvania Law Review PENNumbra, Vol. 156, p. 188, 2007.

[13] <http://www.npr.org/blogs/itsallpolitics/2013/02/06/171301128/even-in-blue-minnesota-gun-control-seems-a-tough-sell> . David Welna. February 6th, 2013. "Even in Blue Minnesota, gun control seems a tough sell."

[14] <http://www.usatoday.com/story/money/business/2013/09/18/starbucks-coffee-guns-ceo-schultz/2829937/ >, "Starbucks CEO says guns not welcome in stores", USA Today, Bruce Horovitz, September 18th, 2013.

[15] <http://www.cnn.com/2012/07/31/politics/gun-ownership-declining/index.html> , Allison Brennan, July 31st, 2012. "Analysis: fewer U.S. gun owners own more guns." Data collected by The Injury Prevention Journal, The UN Office on Drugs and Crime, The General Social Survey and population figures from the US Census Bureau.

16 <http://www.pewresearch.org/fact-tank/2013/06/04/a-minority-of-americans-own-guns-but-just-how-many-is-unclear/> Drew Desilver. June 4th, 2013. 37% of households ad an adult who owned a gun; 24% claimed to own a gun, while 13% said that someone else owned a gun.

17 <http://www.people-press.org/2013/03/12/section-3-gun-ownership-trends-and-demographics/#who-owns> March 12, 2013. "Why own a gun? Protection is now top reason." Pew Research Center for the People and the Press. 74% of gun owners were men and 82% were white, while 61% are white men, who comprise only 32% of the adult U.S. population

18 <http://www.theatlanticwire.com/politics/2012/12/guns-in-america-statistics/60071/> , Elspeth Reeve, December 17th, 2012. "Some uncomfortable Numbers about Guns in America." The Atlantic Wire. In the West, 60% support restriction, 39% do not. In the Northeast, 67% are in favor, while 31% are not. In the South, 50% oppose, 46% favor, and in the Midwest, 49% want more, 48% do not.

19 <http://www.langerresearch.com/uploads/1145a1GunControl.pdf> , December 17th, 2012, "Many see Societal Issues in CT Shootings: Most back ban on high-capacity clips". Overall 54% favor restrictions.

20 <http://readersupportednews.org/pm-section/78-78/4708-americas-gun-problem> , Last Accessed April 4th, 2013. "Americas gun problem" Lamar Hankins. January 24th, 2011. 75% do not feel safer.

21 http://www.cnn.com/2013/04/11/politics/al-qaeda-video/index.html> Sudip Bhattacharya. April 12th, 2013. "Al Qaeda video surfaces claiming how easy it is to buy guns in U.S."

22 http://america.aljazeera.com/articles/2013/10/19/pro-gun-activistsstagecontroversialrallyatthealamo.html> October 19th, 2013, Aljazeera America. By Carolyn Jones. "Pro-gun activists stage controversial rally at the Alamo."

23

<http://www.scholarsstrategynetwork.org/sites/default/files/ssn_key_findings_cook_on_gun_violence.pdf> Philip J. Cook, Sanford School, Duke University. August 2012. "Worries about safety: The real price of gun violence". See "Gun Violence: The real costs (Oxford University Press, 2000) by Philip J. Cook & Jens Ludwig.

24 ALEC - Americal Legislative Executive Council. A conservative group which produces model legislation for state legislatures. They embrace free markets, limited government and federalism. See <http://en.wikipedia.org/wiki/ALEC> .

25 <http://alecexposed.org/w/images/6/64/7J12-Resolution_on_the_Second_Amendment_to_the_U_Exposed.pdf> , Last Accessed 25th March, 2013. "Resolution on the Second Amendment to the Constitution"

26 <http://www.ncbi.nlm.nih.gov/pmc/articles/PMC1829336/> . Katherine Kaufer Christoffel, MD, MPH. Am J Public Health. 2007 April; 97(4):626-629. "Firearm Injuries: Epidemic Then, Endemic Now"

27 <http://en.wikipedia.org/wiki/Demographics_of_the_United_States> , Last Accessed 25th March, 2013.

28 <http://www.gunpolicy.org/firearms/region/united-states> , Last Accessed 26th March, 2013.

29 <http://www.who.int/water_sanitation_health/dwq/iwachap10.pdf> Paul R. Hunter and Lorna Fewtrell. "Acceptable Risk". World Health Organization. Last accessed October 12th, 2013.

30 <http://www.ncbi.nlm.nih.gov/pmc/articles/PMC1829336/> . Katherine Kaufer Christoffel, MD, MPH. Am J Public Health. 2007 April; 97(4):626-629. "Firearm Injuries: Epidemic Then, Endemic Now"

---

[31] <http://www.gunpolicy.org/firearms/region/united-states> , Last Accessed 26th March, 2013.

[32] Bureau of Alcohol, Tobacco, Firearms and Explosives. August 1st 2012. Referenced by article by ABC News, August 25th, 2012. "Guns in America, a statistical look." <http://abcnews.go.com/blogs/headlines/2012/08/guns-in-america-a-statistical-look/>

[33] TD LINX/Nielsen via National Associations of Convenience Stores, The Association for Convenience and Fuel Retailing. Referenced by article: ABC News, August 25th, 2012. "Guns in America, a statistical look." According to >http://www.fueleconomy.gov/feg/quizzes/answerQuiz16.shtml> there are 168,000 gas stations in the U.S.

[34] <http://www.fmi.org/research-resources/supermarket-facts> . "Supermarket Facts" Industry Overview 2011-2012. Last Accessed June 18th, 2013.

[35]

<http://www.aboutmcdonalds.com/content/dam/AboutMcDonalds/Investors/Investors%2
02012/2011%20Annual%20Report%20Final.pdf> . last accessed October 11th, 2013.

[36] ABC News, August 25th, 2012. "Guns in America, a statistical look."

[37] <http://www.ojjdp.gov/pubs/gun_violence/sect01.html> . "Gun violence in the United States: The nature of the problem and current trends". Last Accessed June 19th, 2013.

[38] <http://www.ojjdp.gov/pubs/gun_violence/sect01.html> . "Gun violence in the United States: The nature of the problem and current trends". Last Accessed June 19th, 2013.

[39] <http://www.bjs.gov/content/pub/press/fshbopc0510pr.cfm > Thursday November 8, 2012. Bureau of Justice Statistics.

[40] <http://www.mayorsagainstillegalguns.org/html/local/lost-stolen.shtml> . "Reporting lost and stolen guns". Mayors Against Illegal Guns. Last accessed October 12th, 2013.

[41] Bureau of Alcohol, Firearms, Tobacco and Explosives.

[42] <https://www.atf.gov/sites/default/files/assets/Firearms/chap1.pdf> "Following the gun: Enforcing federal laws against firearms traffickers." June 2000.

[43] <http://www.mayorsagainstillegalguns.org/downloads/pdf/inside-straw-purchases.pdf> Accessed October 14th, 2013. "Inside straw purchasing: How criminals get guns illegally". Mayors Against Illegal Guns.

[44] <http://www.mayorsagainstillegalguns.org/downloads/pdf/inside-straw-purchases.pdf> Accessed October 14th, 2013. "Inside straw purchasing: How criminals get guns illegally". Mayors Against Illegal Guns.

[45] <http://www.mayorsagainstillegalguns.org/downloads/pdf/inside-straw-purchases.pdf> Accessed October 14th, 2013. "Inside straw purchasing: How criminals get guns illegally". Mayors Against Illegal Guns.

[46] <http://www.presidency.ucsb.edu/ws/?pid=58366>, April 12th, 2000. "William J. Clinton Remarks at MSNBC's Townhall Meeting on guns in Denver."

[47] U.S. Department of Treasury, Bureau of Alcohol, Tobacco, Firearms, and Explosives, U.S. Department of Justice joint report: Gun Shows: Brady Checks and Crime Gun Traces, January 1999.

[48] <https://www.atf.gov/sites/default/files/assets/Firearms/chap1.pdf> "Following the gun: Enforcing federal laws against firearms traffickers." June 2000.

[49] ibid.

[50] <http://www.justice.gov/oig/reports/ATF/e0707/final.pdf> "Investigative operations at gun shows". The Bureau of Alcohol, Tobacco, Firearms and Explosives. June 2007.

[51] <http://www.nyc.gov/html/om/pdf/2009/pr442-09_report.pdf> "Gun show undercover: Report on illegal sales at gun shows". October 2009.

[52] ibid.

[53] <http://content.thirdway.org/publications/7/AGS_Report_-_No_Questions_Asked_-

_Background_Checks_Gun_Shows_and_Crime.pdf>. Americans for Gun Safety Foundation. April 2001. "Background checks, gun shows and crime."

[54] <http://en.wikipedia.org/wiki/Gun_shows_in_the_United_States> Last accessed October 15th, 2013.

[55] <http://californiaacep.org/wp-content/uploads/Wintemute-preventing-firearm-violence-what-does-the-research-show-final.pdf> Garen Wintemute, MD, MPH. UC Davis School of Medicine Violence Prevention Research Program. January 29th, 2013.

[56] <http://abcnews.go.com/Business/story?id=7297745#.UcIhefnUlbM> . Nariah Halliwell. April 9th, 2009. "Easy Access: $5000 and one hour buys 10 guns."

[57] <http://injuryprevention.bmj.com/content/early/2012/06/22/injuryprev-2011-040290.abstract > Vittes KA, Vernick JS, Webster DW. Legal status and source of offenders' firearms in states with the least stringent criteria for gun ownership. *Injury Prevention* 2012; Epub.

[58] < http://www.ncbi.nlm.nih.gov/pubmed/9875875> Wintemute GJ, Drake CM, Beaumont JJ, Wright MA. Prior misdemeanor convictions as a risk factor for later violent and firearm-related criminal activity among authorized purchasers of handguns. *JAMA* 1998;280:2083-7.

[59] "The case for gun policy reforms in America". Johns Hopkins Center for Gun Policy and Research. <http://www.jhsph.edu/research/centers-and-institutes/johns-hopkins-center-for-gun-policy-and-research/publications/WhitePaper102512_CGPR.pdf>.

[60] <http://www.nyc.gov/portal/site/nycgov/> . "Mayor Bloomberg announces results of first ever national investigation into illegal online gun sales." December 14th, 2011.

[61] < http://www.bloomberg.com/news/print/2012-12-24/guns-for-sale-websites-show-ease-of-acquiring-firearms.html > . Alison Vekshin, Edvard Patterson. December 24th, 2012. "Guns for sale websites show ease of acquiring firearms."

[62] < http://www.bloomberg.com/news/print/2012-12-24/guns-for-sale-websites-show-ease-of-acquiring-firearms.html > . Alison Vekshin, Edvard Patterson. December 24th, 2012. "Guns for sale websites show ease of acquiring firearms."

[63] <http://www.ncbi.nlm.nih.gov/pmc/articles/PMC2563465/> "The criminal purchase of firearm ammunition". Inj Prev. 2006 October; 12(5):308-311. Accessed October 14th, 2013.

[64] ibid.

[65] Data by the Centers for Disease Control.

[66] Centers for Disease Control and Prevention. Web-based Injury Statistics Query and Reporting System (WISQARS) [Online]. (2003). National Center for Injury Prevention and Control, Centers for Disease Control and Prevention (producer). Available from: URL: www.cdc.gov/injury/wisqars. [2018 February (abbreviated) 23].

[67] <http://www.upenn.edu/ldi/issuebrief11_2.pdf> . Jean Lemaire, PhD, University of Pennsylvania, Leonard Davis Institute of Health Economics.

[68] < http://www.infoplease.com/ipa/A0764212.html>. Source Centers for Disease Control and Prevention, National Vital Statistics Reports, vol. 54, No. 13, Apr 19, 2006.

[69] <http://en.wikipedia.org/wiki/United_States_military_casualties_of_war> . United States military casualties of war. Last Accessed June 6th, 2013.

[70] http://en.wikipedia.org/wiki/Rwanda_genocide , Last Accessed April 3rd, 2013. "Rwandan Genocide."

[71] < http://en.wikipedia.org/wiki/Spanish_Civil_War>. Last Accessed June 12th, 2013.

[72] <http://www.bradycampaign.org/media/press/view/289> . December 30th, 1999. This page has since been removed. It is difficult to verify this data through any authoritative source.

[73] <http://en.wikipedia.org/wiki/Killing_Fields> , Last Accessed April 3rd, 2013. Killing

Fields.

[74] While it is difficult to estimate the number of people killed in the Holocaust, the generally accepted figures are around 6 million Jewish people and 5 million non-Jewish people.

[75] <http://en.wikipedia.org/wiki/United_States_military_casualties_of_war> . Last Accessed June 12th, 2013.

[76] <http://en.wikipedia.org/wiki/United_States_military_casualties_of_war> . Last Accessed June 12th, 2013.

[77] <http://en.wikipedia.org/wiki/United_States_military_casualties_of_war>. Last Accessed June 12th, 2013.

[78] < http://www.cdc.gov/injury/wisqars/index.html> Last accessed October 15th, 2013. Fatal Injury Data, Fatal injury Reports. Select by homicide/firearm/state.

[79] <http://www.uphs.upenn.edu/ficap/resourcebook/pdf/monograph.pdf> , Last Accessed April 4th, 2013. "Firearm Injury in the U.S.". Firearm Injury Center at Penn

[80] <http://www.dailykos.com/story/2012/12/14/1169385/-CDC-statistics-show-that-gun-violence-is-not-decreasing> , By distraught. December 14th, 2012. Figures from the Centers for Disease Control

[81] <http://www.dailykos.com/story/2012/12/14/1169385/-CDC-statistics-show-that-gun-violence-is-not-decreasing> , By distraught. December 14th, 2012. Figures from the Centers for Disease Control

[82] <http://www.dailykos.com/story/2012/12/14/1169385/-CDC-statistics-show-that-gun-violence-is-not-decreasing> , By distraught. December 14th, 2012. Figures from the Centers for Disease Control

[83] Centers for Disease Control and Prevention. Web-based Injury Statistics Query and Reporting System (WISQARS) [Online]. (2003). National Center for Injury Prevention and Control, Centers for Disease Control and Prevention (producer). Available from: URL: www.cdc.gov/injury/wisqars. [2018 February (abbreviated) 23].

[84] <http://www.dailykos.com/story/2012/12/14/1169385/-CDC-statistics-show-that-gun-violence-is-not-decreasing> , By distraught. December 14th, 2012. Figures from the Centers for Disease Control

[85] Centers for Disease Control and Prevention. Web-based Injury Statistics Query and Reporting System (WISQARS) [Online]. (2003). National Center for Injury Prevention and Control, Centers for Disease Control and Prevention (producer). Available from: URL: www.cdc.gov/injury/wisqars. [2018 February (abbreviated) 23].

[86] <http://www.dailykos.com/story/2012/12/14/1169385/-CDC-statistics-show-that-gun-violence-is-not-decreasing> , By distraught. December 14th, 2012. Figures from the Centers for Disease Control

[87] < http://articles.latimes.com/1998/apr/17/news/mn-40311>. Associated Press. April 17th, 1998. Sourced from the Centers for Disease Control and the International Journal of Epidemiology

[88] Harvard School of Public Health, Journal of Trauma, 2000. "Firearm availability and homicide rates across 26 high-income countries." David Hemnway, PhD. Matthew Miller, MD, SPH, ScD.

[89] Social Science and Medicine, 2007.

[90] American Journal of Public Health, 2002.

[91] <http://www.hsph.harvard.edu/hicrc/firearms-research/gun-threats-and-self-defense-gun-use/> . Accident Analysis and Prevention, 2001. Harvard Injury Control Research Center. **Miller, Matthew; Azrael, Deborah; Hemenway, David.** Firearm availability and unintentional firearm deaths. *Accident Analysis and Prevention.* 2001; 33:477-84.

[92] National Vital Statistics Reports. December 29th, 2011. "Deaths: Final data for 2009."

[93] http://www.jstor.org/discover/10.2307/1602740 . Philip J. Cook, Jens Ludwig. The

future of children, Vol 12, No. 2, Children, Youth and Gun Violence (Summer - Autumn, 2202), pp 86-99.

[94] <http://jama.jamanetwork.com/article.aspx?articleid=191001> Philip J. Cook et al. *JAMA.* 1999;282(5):447-454. doi:10.1001/jama.282.5.447 "The medical costs of gunshot injuries in the United States

[95] <http://www.phc4.org/reports/researchbriefs/080405/nr080405.htm> Pennsylvania Healthcare Cost Containment Council. "Firearm related injuries in Pennsylvania". August 2005.

[96] <http://knowledge.wpengine.com/wp-content/uploads/2013/09/1294.pdf> Jean Lamaire. Wharton School, University of Pennsylvania.

[97] < http://www.lao.ca.gov/laoapp/laomenus/sections/crim_justice/6_cj_inmatecost.aspx?catid=3>. "Californias annual costs to incarcerate an inmate in prison." 2008-09. Legislative Analysts Office.

[98] < http://www.nytimes.com/2013/08/24/nyregion/citys-annual-cost-per-inmate-is-nearly-168000-study-says.html?_r=0>. Marc Santora. August 23rd, 2013. "City's annual cost per inmate is $168,000, Study finds."

[99] <http://www.seattlepi.com/national/article/Gun-violence-costs-nation-100-billion-a-year-1265606.php> . Joanne Loviglio, The Associated Press. February 26th, 2008. "Gun Violence costs nation $100 Billion a year"

[100] <http://www.huffingtonpost.com/john-rosenthal/health-care-costs-and-gun_b_393054.html>. John Rosenthal. December 15, 2009. "Health care costs and gun violence."

[101] Public Services Research Institute, 2008.

[102] Philip Cook, Duke University, Jens Ludwig, University of Chicago.

[103] <http://en.wikipedia.org/wiki/United_States_cities_by_crime_rate> . Last Accessed June 24th, 2013.

[104] < http://www.freep.com/article/20130305/FEATURES01/130305010/Gun-violence-annual-cost-12-billion>.>. Kelly Kennedy, USA Today March 5th, 2013. Study author Ted Miller. Study with funding by the National Institute of Justice, 1992

[105] Small Arms Survey, 2006, Chapter 8.

[106] Cook PJ, Ludwig J. *Gun Violence: the Real Costs.* New York: Oxford University Press, 2000.

[107] <http://www.smallarmssurvey.org/publications/by-type/yearbook/small-arms-survey-2006.html> Small Arms Survey, 2006, Chapter 8. "The instrument matters: Assessing the costs of small arms violence."

[108] < http://papers.ssrn.com/sol3/papers.cfm?abstract_id=782994 > Lemaire J. The cost of firearm deaths in the United States: reduced life expectancies and increased insurance costs. *Journal of Risk and Insurance.* 2005;72:359-374.

[109] Lemaire J. The cost of firearm deaths n the United States: reduced life expectancies and increased insurance costs. *Journal of Risk and Insurance.* 2005;72:359-374.

[110] < http://www.visionofhumanity.org/#/page/indexes/global-peace-index> 2012 United States Peace Index. Institute for Economics and Peace.

[111] <http://futureofchildren.org/futureofchildren/publications/docs/12_02_06.pdf> Philip J. Cook & Jens Ludwig. "The costs of gun violence against children." Accessed October 17th, 2013.

[112] <http://www.smallarmssurvey.org/publications/by-type/yearbook.html> Small Arms Survey, 2006, Chapter 8.

[113] < http://en.wikipedia.org/wiki/Jeff_Cooper> Grossman, Arnold. *One Nation Under Guns: An Essay on an American Epidemic*, Fulcrum Publishing, 2006 ISBN 9781555915575 (p. 65).

Accessed October 17th, 2013.

[114] <http://www.americanprogress.org/issues/race/news/2013/01/17/49885/top-10-reasons-why-communities-of-color-should-care-about-stricter-gun-violence-prevention-laws/> . Morriah Kaplan, Sophia Kerby. January 17th, 2013. "Top 10 reasons why communities of color should care about stricter gun-violence prevention laws."

[115] < http://www.cdc.gov/nchs/deaths.htm> Mortality Data. National Vital Statistics Reports, Vol 59, No. 10, December 7, 2011.

[116] Cook, Philip J., Jens Ludwig (2000). "Chapter 2". *Gun Violence: The Real Costs*. Oxford University Press.ISBN 0-19-513793-0. Referred by < http://en.wikipedia.org/wiki/Gun_violence_in_the_United_States> Last accessed October 17th, 2013.

[117] < http://en.wikipedia.org/wiki/Gun_violence_in_the_United_States>. Accessed October 17th, 2013.

[118] Study at the Vanderbilt Medical Center in Nashville. <http://www.jem-journal.com/article/S0736-4679(12)00880-3/abstract>. Journal of Emergency Medicine. Volume 44. Issue 3. pp 585-591. March 2013.

[119] <http://www.advances.umn.edu/2013/04/a-public-health-response-to-gun-violence/>. John Finnegan, Dean, University of Minnesota School of Public Health. July 20th, 2013. "A public health response to gun violence."

[120] The future of children Volume 12 - Number 2 Summer/Fall 2002. "Children, youth and gun violence."

[121] <http://www.fbi.gov/>. Uniform Crime Reports.

[122] "Gun Control", Opposing Viewpoints Series, 2007, Thomson Gale.

[123] < http://aje.oxfordjournals.org/content/160/10/929.full>. Linda L Dahlberg, Robin M. Ikeda, Marcie-jo Kresnow. "American Journal of Epidemiology, Vol 160, Issue 10, pp 929-936. "Guns in the home and risk of a violent death in the home: Findings from a national study."

[124] < http://aje.oxfordjournals.org/content/160/10/929.full>. American Journal of Epidemiology, Vol 160, Issue 10 pp929-936. Linda L Dahlberg, Robin M Ikeda, Marcie-jo Kresnow. "Guns in the home and risk of a violent death in the home:findings from a national study."

[125] < http://www.nejm.org/doi/pdf/10.1056/NEJM199208133270705 > Kellermann AL, Rivara FP, Somes G, et al. "Suicide in the home in relation to gun ownership". N Engl J Med 1992;327:467–72.

[126] <http://www.ncbi.nlm.nih.gov/pubmed/12764330> Wiebe DJ. Violence Prevention Research Group, University of California-Los Angeles School of Public Health. "Homicide and suicide risks with firearms in the home: a national case-control study"

[127] <http://www.nejm.org/doi/full/10.1056/NEJM199310073291506> Kellerman, Arthur L. et al. "Gun ownership as a risk factor for homicide in the home."

[128] <http://www.washingtonpost.com/wp-dyn/content/article/2008/06/27/AR2008062702864.html> Arthur Kellerman. Washington Post. June 29th, 2008. "Guns for safety? Dream on, Scalia."

[129] <http://www.ncbi.nlm.nih.gov/pubmed/9715182> Journal of Trauma, 1998.

[130] < http://www.medscape.com/viewarticle/717278 > Southern Medical Journal, journal of the Southern Medical Association. Dr. Stephen Lippman et al. South Med J. 2010;103(2):151-153. "Do guns provide safety? At what cost?

[131] < http://arstechnica.com/science/2011/04/guns-in-the-home-lots-of-risk-ambiguity/>. John Timmer. April 27th, 2011. "Guns at home more likely to be used stupidly than in self-defense." Data based on studies by David Hemenway, Harvard School of Public

Health.
[132] <http://ajl.sagepub.com/content/early/2011/02/01/1559827610396294>. February 1st, 2011. "Risks and benefits of a gun in the home." David Hemenway, Ph.D.
[133] < http://aje.oxfordjournals.org/content/160/10/929.full>. American Journal of Epidemiology, Vol 160, Issue 10 pp929-936. Linda L Dahlberg, Robin M Ikeda, Marciejo Kresnow. "Guns in the home and risk of a violent death in the home:findings from a national study."
[134] <http://ajl.sagepub.com/content/early/2011/02/01/1559827610396294> . February 1st, 2011. "Risks and benefits of a gun in the home." David Hemenway, Ph.D.
[135] < http://ajl.sagepub.com/content/early/2011/02/01/1559827610396294> . February 1st, 2011. "Risks and benefits of a gun in the home." David Hemenway, Ph.D.
[136] < http://ajl.sagepub.com/content/early/2011/02/01/1559827610396294> . February 1st, 2011. "Risks and benefits of a gun in the home." David Hemenway, Ph.D
[137] <http://www.gao.gov/products/PEMD-91-9>. U.S. General Accounting Office. "Accidental shootings: Many deaths and injuries caused by firearms could have been prevented." GAO/PEMD-91-9. Washington, DC: GAO, March 1991.
[138] < http://www.huffingtonpost.com/2013/05/04/nra-speaker-gun-safes-kids-bedrooms-home-defense_n_3216157.html>. Meredith Bennett Smith. May 4th, 2013. "NRA convention speaker Rob Pincus advises keeping gun safes in kids' bedrooms for self defense."
[139] <http://pediatrics.aappublications.org/content/107/6/1247>. Jackman, G.A., Farah, M.M., Kellermann, A.L., et al. "Seeing is believing: What do boys do when they find a real gun?" *Pediatrics* (June 2001) 107(6):1247–50. .
[140] <http://www.childrensdefense.org/child-research-data-publications/data/protect-children-not-guns-2012.html>. "Protect children not guns." Last accessed July 1st, 2013. Frances Baxley and Matthew Miller. 2006. "Parental Misconceptions about Children and Firearms." Archives of Pediatrics and Adolescent Medicine, 160(5): 542-547. Also see < http://archpedi.jamanetwork.com/article.aspx?articleid=204929>.
[141] <http://www.ncbi.nlm.nih.gov/pubmed/11026174>. Brent, D.A., Baugher, M., Birmaher, B., et al. Compliance with recommendations to remove firearms in families participating in a clinical trial for adolescent depression. *Journal of the American Academy of Child and Adolescent Psychiatry* (October 2000) 39(10):1220–26.
[142] Centers for Disease Control and Prevention. <http://webappa.cdc.gov/sasweb/ncipc/mortrate10_us.html>.
[143] <http://www.stophandgunviolence.com/facts.asp>. Last Accessed June 19th, 2013. Also see <http://www.fbi.gov/about-us/cjis/ucr/leoka/leoka-2010>
[144] <http://www.princeton.edu/futureofchildren/publications/docs/12_02_01_.pdf> "Children, youth and gun violence:Analysis and Recommendations". Reich, Kathleen. Culross, Patti L. Behrman, Richard E. Volume 12 Number 2 Summer/Fall 2002. U.S. Department of Justice, March 2000.
[145] <http://www.childrensdefense.org/child-research-data-publications/data/state_data-repository/protect-children-not-guns-key-facts-2013.pdf>. April 24th, 2013
[146] <http://www.cdc.gov/injury/wisqars/nonfatal.html>. WISQARS Injury prevention and control: Data and statistics.
[147] < http://www.nasponline.org/resources/crisis_safety/Youth_Gun_Violence_Fact_Sheet.pdf >. National Association of School Psychologists. "Youth gun violence fact sheet.". 2012.
[148] <http://www.cdc.gov/mmwr/preview/mmwrhtml/00046149.htm> "Rates of Homicide, Suicide, and Firearm-Related Death Among Children -- 26 Industrialized Countries," Morbidity and Mortality Weekly Report 46(05): 101-105, February 07, 1997. Centers for

Disease Control and Prevention.

[149] Fingerhut LA, Cox CS, Warner M et al. International comparative analysis of injury mortality: findings from the ICE on injury statistics. *Advance Data from Vital and Health Statistics; 303*. Hyattsville, Maryland: National Center for Health Statistics. 1998.

[150] <http://www.stophandgunviolence.com/facts.asp> Harborview Injury Prevention and Research Center Study, Archives of Pediatric and Adolescent Medicine, August 1999.

[151] <http://www.ncbi.nlm.nih.gov/pubmed/14977275>. Freed HA, Milzman DP, Holt RW, Wang A. "Age 14 starts a child's increased risk of major knife or gun injury in Washington D.C. February 2004.

[152] <http://thinkprogress.org/health/2013/07/12/2291811/cdc-guns-kids-murdered/> . Tara Culp-Ressler. July 12th, 2013. "Federal health officials warn the number of kids getting murdered by guns is rising."

[153] < http://sbcoalition.org/category/reports-and-statistics/ > Pediatrics, 2012: 130(5):e1416-e1423. "Guns continue to kill American children".Coalition against gun violence.

[154] <http://thinkprogress.org/health/2013/07/12/2291811/cdc-guns-kids-murdered/> . Tara Culp-Ressler. July 12th, 2013. "Federal health officials warn the number of kids getting murdered by guns is rising."

[155] <http://thinkprogress.org/health/2013/07/12/2291811/cdc-guns-kids-murdered/> . Tara Culp-Ressler. July 12th, 2013. "Federal health officials warn the number of kids getting murdered by guns is rising."

[156] <http://www.uphs.upenn.edu/ficap/resourcebook/pdf/monograph.pdf> , Last Accessed April 5th, 2013. "Firearm Injury in the U.S.". "U.S. Youth Firearm Deaths Compared to Other Causes, 2007.

[157] CDC, National Center for Injury Prevention and Control, Ten Leading Causes of Death, United States, 1993-1995. Rev. 7/7/98; CDC/National Center for Health Statistics, 1997; State of California, Department of Health Services, Death Records, Table 02 Death By Age 1-19, Sex and Cause of Death (1996). - See more at: http://corporate.findlaw.com/litigation-disputes/city-lawsuits-against-gun-industry-will-pressure-firearm.html#_ftn2

[158] <http://www.psychologytoday.com/blog/wired-success/201212/gun-control-and-the-culture-violence>, Ray Williams. First published in "Wired for Success.". December 17th, 2012.

[159] <http://www.rand.org/pubs/research_briefs/RB4535.html>. Schuster, M.A., Franke, T.M., Bastian, A.M., et al. Firearm storage patterns in US homes with children. *American Journal of Public Health* (April 2000) 90(4):588–94.

[160] ibid.

[161] ibid.

[162] <http://www.med.umich.edu/yourchild/topics/guns.htm> University of Michigan Health System. June 12th, 2013. "Gun Safety for kids and Youth".

[163] <http://www.ncbi.nlm.nih.gov/pubmed/8856516>. Hardy, M.S., Armstrong, F.D., Martin, B.L., et al. A firearm safety program for children: They just can't say no. *Developmental and Behavioral Pediatrics* (August 1996) 17(4):216–21.

[164] <https://www.ncjrs.gov/pdffiles1/ojjdp/188992.pdf>. Lizotte, A., and Sheppard, D. *Gun use by male juveniles: Research and prevention.* Washington, DC: U.S. Department of Justice, Office of Justice Programs, Office of Juvenile Justice and Delinquency Prevention, July 2001.

[165] http://www.blackyouthproject.com/2012/03/report-gun-homicide-is-the-leading-cause-of-death-among-black-teens/ . "Report: gun homicide is the leading cause of death among black teens.". March 28th, 2012. BYP. Also see

<http://www.cdc.gov/injury/wisqars/leading_causes_death.html>
[166] < http://www.nejm.org/doi/full/10.1056/NEJMp1215606>. Judith S Palfrey, M.D. Sean Palfrey, M.D. N Engl J Med 2013; 368:401-403. DOI: 10.1056/NEJMp1215606. January 31st, 2013. "Preventing gun deaths in children".
[167] <http://www.ncbi.nlm.nih.gov/pubmed/15554803 >. Buckner, J. C., Beardslee, W. R. and Bassuk, E. L. (2004), Exposure to Violence and Low-Income Children's Mental Health: Direct, Moderated, and Mediated Relations. American Journal of Orthopsychiatry, 74: 413–423. doi: 10.1037/0002-9432.74.4.413
[168] < http://www.ncbi.nlm.nih.gov/pubmed/11732955 >. Hurt, H., Malmud, E., Brodsky, N.L., and Giannetta, J. Exposure to violence: Psychological and academic correlates in child witnesses. *Archives of Pediatrics and Adolescent Medicine* December 2001) 155(12):1351–56.
[169]
<http://www.nasponline.org/resources/crisis_safety/Youth_Gun_Violence_Fact_Sheet.pd f>. "Youth gun violence fact sheet. National Association of School Psychologists. Data from the Centers for Disease Control, 2012.
[170] <http://www.ncbi.nlm.nih.gov/pubmed/6876209>. Harris W, Luterman A, Curreri PW. "BB and Pellet guns - toys or deadly weapons." July 1983.
[171] Centers for Disease Control and Prevention, Youth Risk Behavior Study, 1997.
[172] <http://eric.ed.gov/?id=ED368838>. J.F. Sheley and J.D. Wright, *Gun Acquisition and Possession in Selected Juvenile Samples*, Research in Brief, Washington, DC: U.S. Department of Justice, National Institute of Justice, Office of Juvenile Justice and Delinquency Prevention, 1993.
[173] ibid.
[174] <http://www.stophandgunviolence.com/facts.asp>. ATF Crime report, Crime Gun Trace Analysis, February 1999.
[175] < http://www.ncbi.nlm.nih.gov/books/NBK44294/ >. U.S. Department of Health and Human Services. *Youth violence: A report of the Surgeon General*. Rockville, MD: U.S. Department of Health and Human Services, Centers for Disease Control and Prevention, National Center for Injury Prevention and Control, Substance Abuse and Mental Health Services Administration, Center for Mental Health Services; and National Institutes of Health, National Institute of Mental Health, 2001, p. 49.
[176]
<http://www.mayorsagainstillegalguns.org/downloads/pdf/Commerce_in_Firearms_2000 .pdf>. Bureau of Alcohol, Tobacco and Firearms. *Commerce in firearms in the United States*. Washington, DC: ATF, February 2000, p. 2.
[177] <https://www.ncjrs.gov/pdffiles1/nij/217397.pdf>. "Adolescents, neighborhoods and violence: Recent findings from the project on human development in Chicago neighborhoods.". U.S. Department of Justice, National Institute of Justice. p11. article 3.
[178] <http://prospect.org/article/can-we-keep-guns-away-kids>. Kennedy, D. Can we keep guns away from kids? *The American Prospect* (June 23, 1994) 5(18):74–80.
[179] <https://www.ncjrs.gov/pdffiles1/nij/217397.pdf>. "Adolescents, neighborhoods and violence: Recent findings from the project on human development in Chicago neighborhoods". National Institute of Justice. Sept 2007.
[180] <http://crimelab.uchicago.edu/page/report>. "Gun violence among school age youth in Chicago." March 2009. Roseanna Ander, Philip J Cook, Jens Ludwig, Harold Pollack.
[181] <http://www.thedailybeast.com/articles/2012/06/13/spike-in-shootings-murders-creates-wild-wild-midwest-effect-in-chicago.html>, Michael Daly. June 13th, 2012. "Spike in Shootings, Murders, creates 'Wild, Wild Midwest Effect in Chicago".
[182] <http://www.thedailybeast.com/articles/2012/06/13/spike-in-shootings-murders-

creates-wild-wild-midwest-effect-in-chicago.html>, Michael Daly. June 13th, 2012. "Spike in Shootings, Murders, creates 'Wild, Wild Midwest Effect in Chicago".

[183] < http://pricetheory.uchicago.edu/levitt/Papers/CullenLevittCrimeUrban1999.pdf >. Cullen, Julie Berry, Levitt, Steven D "Crime, Urban Flight and the consequences for cities." The Review of Economics and statistics. Vol LXXXI, May 1999, Number 2.

[184] <http://www.marketplace.org/topics/wealth-poverty/guns-and-dollars/economic-costs-violence-chicago>. Sylvester Monroe. "The economic costs of violence in Chicago." February 11th, 2013.

[185] <http://www.nytimes.com/2013/05/06/us/kentucky-town-rejects-girls-gun-death-as-a-symbol.html?_r=0>. Trip Gabriel. May 5th, 2013. "Girl's death by gunshot is rejected as symbol."

[186] <http://www.crickett.com/crickett_aboutus.php>. Last accessed July 1st, 2013.

[187] < http://www.nejm.org/doi/full/10.1056/NEJMp0805923>. Matthew Miller, M.D., Sc.D & David Hemenway, Ph.D. September 4th, 2008. "Guns and suicides in the United States." N Engl J Med 2008; 359:989-991. DOI: 10.1056/NEJMp0805923

[188] <http://ajl.sagepub.com/content/early/2011/02/01/1559827610396294> . February 1st, 2011. "Risks and benefits of a gun in the home." David Hemenway, Ph.D. Extracts from "Household firearm ownership and rates of suicide across the 50 U.S. states. Miller M, Lippman S, Azrael D, Hemenway D. J. Trauma. 2007;62:1029-1035.

[189] <http://www.ncbi.nlm.nih.gov/pubmed/14729556> Oslin DW et al. "Managing suicide risk in late life: access to firearms as a public health risk." Am J Geriatr Psychiatry 2004 Jan-Feb;12(1):30-6.

[190] < http://futureofchildren.org/publications/journals/>. The future of children Volume 12 - Number 2 Summer/Fall 2002. "Children, youth and gun violence." Also see <http://www.cdc.gov/injury/wisqars/index.html>

[191] United Nations Office on Drugs and Crime. See <http://www.gunpolicy.org/>

[192] < http://www.childrensdefense.org/child-research-data-publications/> . April 24th, 2013. "Protect children not guns 2013."

[193] < http://www.ncbi.nlm.nih.gov/pubmed/17965940>. Clark C et al. J Urban Health. 2008 Jan;85(1):22-38. Epub 2007 Oct 27. "Witnessing community violence in residential neighborhoods: a mental health hazard for urban women."

[194] <http://www.ncbi.nlm.nih.gov/pmc/articles/PMC2704268/>. Johnson Sarah Lindstrom et al. J Urban Health. 2009 July; 86(4): 538–550. "Neighborhood violence and its association with mothers health: Assessing the relative importance of perceived safety and exposure to violence."

[195] <http://16dayscwgl.rutgers.edu/component/docman/doc_view/441-domestic-violence-a-small-armspdf >. Domestic Violence and Small Arms. Rutgers Center for Women's Global Leadership.

[196] < http://www.sciencedaily.com/releases/2011/04/110427101532.htm >. "Guns in the home provide greater health risk than benefit." April 28th, 2011. Data based on studies by David Hemenway, Harvard School of Public Health.

[197] <http://www.jhsph.edu/research/centers-and-institutes/johns-hopkins-center-for-gun-policy-and-research/publications/IPV_Guns.pdf>. "Intimate partner violence and firearms. Last accessed July 3rd, 2013. Johns Hopkins Bloomberg school of public health. Center for gun policy and research..

[198]

<http://www.ifvcc.org/illinoisfirearms/advocatechecklists/Advocate%20Reference%20Guide.pdf>. Last accessed july 2nd, 2013. "Domestic Violence and Firearms: An advocates guide". The Illinois Family violence coordinating councils - firearms and domestic violence project. 2008.

199 <http://16dayscwgl.rutgers.edu/component/docman/doc_view/441-domestic-violence-a-small-armspdf >. Domestic Violence and Small Arms. Rutgers Center for Women's Global Leadership

200 <http://www.futureswithoutviolence.org/userfiles/file/Children_and_Families/Guns.pdf>. "The facts on guns and domestic violence.". Futures without violence. Last accessed July 3rd, 2013.

201 <http://www.vpc.org/studies/myth.htm>. "A deadly myth: Women, handguns and self-defense." Violence Policy Center. Last accessed August 15th, 2013.

202 <http://www.vpc.org/studies/wmmw2012.pdf>. "When men murder women - an analysis of 2010 homicide data." September 2012. The Violence Policy Center.

203 < http://www.futureswithoutviolence.org/ >. "The facts on women, children and gun violence". Futures Without Violence.

204 Fox JA. Zawitz MW. Homicide trends in the U.S.: Intimate homicides. Washington, DC: Bureau of Justice Statistics, Office of Justice Programs, U.S. Department of Justice; 2007.

205 Tjaden P. Thoennes N. Prevalence, incidence and consequences of violence against women: Findings from the National Violence Against Women Survey. Research in Brief from National Institute of Justice and the Centers for Disease Control and Prevention. Washington, DC: U. S. Department of Justice; 1998.

206 < http://www.ncbi.nlm.nih.gov/pmc/articles/PMC1447915/ > Campbell JC. Webster D. Koziol-McLain J, et al. Risk factors for femicide in abusive relationships: Results from a mulitsite case control study. Am J Public Health. 2003;93:1089–1097.

207 <http://www.ncbi.nlm.nih.gov/pmc/articles/PMC1448464/> Susan B Sorenson, PhD and Douglas J. Wiebe, PhD.August 2004. "Weapons in the lives of battered women."

208 <http://controlarms.org/wordpress/wp-content/uploads/2011/02/The-Impact-of-Guns-on-Womens-Lives.pdf>. Last Accessed July 4th, 2013. Amnesty International, the International Action Network on Small Arms (IANSA) and Oxfam International in 2005.

209 < http://nocera.blogs.nytimes.com/2013/05/09/the-gun-report-may-9-2013/>. May 9th, 2013. Joe Nocera. "The gun report: May 9th, 2013". See <http://houston.cbslocal.com/2013/05/07/nra-convention-vendor-sells-bleeding-female-mannequin-target-called-the-ex/> "NRA convention vendor sells bleeding female mannequin target called 'The Ex'." CBS. May 7th, 2013.

210 <http://academic.udayton.edu/health/01status/01noll.htm>. Linda J Noll. University of Dayton Third year law student. Last accessed December 5th, 2013. Also see <http://www.seiu.org/2009/09/domestic-violence-victims-have-a-pre-existing-condition.php>. September 11th, 2009. Maria Tchijov.

211 <http://www.womenslawproject.org/brochures/Insurance_discrimDV.pdf>. Insurance discrimination against victims of domestic violence. The Pennsylvania Coalition Against Domestic Violence and the Women's Law Project. Last accessed December 5th, 2013.

212 <http://www.nytimes.com/2013/03/18/us/facing-protective-orders-and-allowed-to-keep-guns.html>. Michael Luo. March 17th, 2013. "In some states, gun rights trump orders of protection."

213 <http://www.ncbi.nlm.nih.gov/pubmed/23759665>. Katherine W Vittes et al. "Removing guns from batterers: findings from a pilot survey of domestic violence restraining order recipients in California." June 12, 2013.

214 ibid.

215 ibid.

216 <http://injuryprevention.bmj.com/content/16/2/90.abstract>. November 29th, 2009. April M Zeoli, Daniel W. Webster. "Effects of domestic violence policies, alcohol taxes

---

and police staffing levels on intimate partner homicide in large cities."
[217] <http://www.nytimes.com/2013/03/18/us/facing-protective-orders-and-allowed-to-keep-guns.html>. Michael Luo. March 17th, 2013. "In some states, gun rights trump orders of protection."
[218] http://www.huffingtonpost.com/2013/03/29/domestic-violence-gun-ban_n_2978673.html . Mat Ferner. March 29th, 2013. "Domestic Violence Gun Ban Bill Passes Colorado House Committee."
[219] <http://libcloud.s3.amazonaws.com/9/56/4/1242/1/analysis-of-recent-mass-shootings.pdf>. Last Accessed July 5th, 2013. "Analysis of recent mass shootings". Mayors Against Illegal Guns.
[220]

<http://www.ncdsv.org/images/MAIG_ConnectionBetweenDVandWeakGunLaws_2013.pdf>. "The connection between domestic violence and weak gun laws". Mayors Against Illegal Guns.
[221] <http://www.fbi.gov/about-us/cjis/nics> . "National Instant Criminal Background Check System".
[222]

<http://www.ncdsv.org/images/MAIG_ConnectionBetweenDVandWeakGunLaws_2013.pdf>. "The connection between domestic violence and weak gun laws." . Last accessed July 3rd, 2013.
[223] http://www.victimsofcrime.org/docs/src/stalking-fact-sheet_english.pdf?sfvrsn=4 . Stalking Resource Center. The National Center for Victims of Crime. "Stalking Fact Sheet.".
[224] <http://controlarms.org/wordpress/wp-content/uploads/2011/02/The-Impact-of-Guns-on-Womens-Lives.pdf>. Last Accessed July 4th, 2013. Amnesty International, the International Action Network on Small Arms (IANSA) and Oxfam International in 2005. "The impact of guns on peoples lives."
[225] <http://www.jhsph.edu/research/centers-and-institutes/johns-hopkins-center-for-gun-policy-and-research/publications/IPV_Guns.pdf>. "Intimate partner violence and firearms. Last accessed July 3rd, 2013. Johns Hopkins Bloomberg school of public health. Center for gun policy and research.
[226] <http://www.amednews.com/article/20120806/health/308069935/4/>. Christine S. Moyer. August 6th, 2012. "Aurora-style rampages can lead to anxiety, depression among the public."
[227] <http://crimelab.uchicago.edu/page/report>. Last accessed June 30th, 2013.
[228]

<http://www.princeton.edu/main/news/archive/S36/98/43S47/index.xml?section=topstories>. Jamie Saxon, Office of Communications. May 29th, 2013. "Forum examines 'epidemic' of gun violence as a public health issue."
[229] ibid.
[230] <http://npalliance.org/blog/2013/05/24/its-time-for-doctors-to-talk-about-guns/>. Becky Martin. May 24th, 2013. "Gun Violence - A public health issue with solutions."
[231] < http://sph.umn.edu/a-public-health-response-to-gun-violence/ > . John Finnegan, Dean, University of Minnesota School of Public Health. July 20th, 2013. "A public health response to gun violence.".
[232] <http://www.al.com/opinion/index.ssf/2013/04/mental_illness_does_not_equal.html>. Marilyn K. Lands, M.S. April 30th, 2013. "Mental illness does not equal gun violence."
[233] <http://www.iom.edu/Activities/PublicHealth/FirearmViolenceReduction.aspx>. Institute of Medicine of the National Academies. Last accessed July 23rd, 2013. "Priorities for a public health research agenda to reduce the threat of firearm-related

violence."
[234] <http://www.cnn.com/2013/04/24/health/kids-guns-study>. Jen Christensen. April 24th, 2013. "Kids and guns: 'These are not isolated tragedies.'"
[235] <http://mediamatters.org/blog/2013/01/18/sorry-rush-gun-violence-is-a-health-care-issue/192320>. Eric Boehlert. January 18th, 2013.
[236] ibid.
[237] <http://www.forbes.com/sites/robwaters/2012/07/24/gun-violence-the-public-health-issue-politicians-want-to-ignore/>. Rob Waters. July 24th, 2012. "Gun Violence: The public health issue politicians want to ignore."
[238] < http://www.huffingtonpost.com/dorothy-stoneman/poverty-gun-violence_b_3528888.html> Dorothy Stoneman, Founder and CEO, YouthBuild USA, Inc. HuffingtonPost. July 1st, 2013.
[239] <http://www.amednews.com/article/20120910/health/309109949/2/>. Christine S Moyer. September 10th, 2012. "Public health approach: Physicians aim to prevent gun violence."
[240] <http://www.amednews.com/article/20080211/health/302119976/4/>. Victoria Stagg Elliott. February 11th, 2008. "Break it down: Drop guns, wear condoms."
[241] <http://www.ncbi.nlm.nih.gov/pubmed/7063294>. Walton WW. March 1982. "An evaluation of the Poison Prevention Packaging Act."
[242] <http://www.ncbi.nlm.nih.gov/pubmed/11787305>. Hemenway D. 2001. "The public health approach to motor vehicles, tobacco and alcohol, with applications to firearms policy.
[243] <http://www.irinnews.org/report/93042/south-africa-aids-conspiracy-believers-less-likely-to-condomise>. "South Africa: AIDS conspiracy believers less likely to compromise.". June 22nd, 2011.
[244] < http://sph.umn.edu/a-public-health-response-to-gun-violence/ > . John Finnegan, Dean, University of Minnesota School of Public Health. July 20th, 2013. "A public health response to gun violence.".
[245] <http://jama.jamanetwork.com/article.aspx?articleid=1556167>. Dariush Mozaffarian, MD, DrPH, David Hemenway, PhD; David S. Ludwig, MD, PhD. February 13th, 2013. "Curbing gun violence: Lessons from public health successes." Original reference: http://www.ncbi.nlm.nih.gov/pubmed/21900875 . Centers for Disease Control and Prevention. September 9th, 2011.
[246] <http://www.sciencedirect.com/science/article/pii/S0047272705000411>. Philip J Cook; Jens Ludwig. January 2006. "The Social Costs of Gun Ownership."
[247] <http://www.ncbi.nlm.nih.gov/pubmed/11787305> . Hemenway D. 2001. "The public health approach to motor vehicles, tobacco and alcohol, with applications to firearms policy."
[248] <http://www1.umn.edu/humanrts/demo/smallarms2003.html>. Specific Human Rights Issues: Prevention of human rights violations committed with small arms and light weapons." Barbara Frey, Special Rapporteur in accordance with Sub-Commission resolution 2002/25.
[249] <www.nytimes.com/2013/06/06/health/panel-urges-better-gathering-of-gun-violence-data.html?_r=0>. Sabrina Tevernise. June 5th, 2013. "Panel says better data is needed on gun issues."
[250] <http://www.browndailyherald.com/2013/04/10/panel-refutes-link-between-mental-illness-and-gun-violence/>. Adam Toobin. April 10th, 2013. "Panel refutes link between mental illness and gun violence."
[251] <http://www.nimh.nih.gov/health/publications/the-numbers-count-mental-disorders-in-america/index.shtml#Intro> . "The numbers count: Mental disorders in America."

National Institute of Mental Health. Last accessed August 21st, 2013.

[252] <http://www.browndailyherald.com/2013/04/10/panel-refutes-link-between-mental-illness-and-gun-violence/>. Adam Toobin. April 10th, 2013. "Panel refutes link between mental illness and gun violence."

[253] <http://harvardpress.typepad.com/hup_publicity/2011/02/misconceptions-madness-mayhem-what-is-mental-illness.html>. February 7th, 2011. "Misconceptions about Madness and Mayhem." Harvard University Press.

[254] <http://www.bmj.com/content/346/bmj.f557>. "Mental disorders and vulnerability to homicidal death: Swedish nationwide cohort study." March 5th, 2013. BMJ 2013;346:f557. Casey Crump, Kristina Sundquist. Marilyn A Winkleby, Jan Sundquist.

[255] <http://www.washingtonpost.com/blogs/wonkblog/wp/2012/12/21/the-nra-wants-an-active-mental-illness-database-thirty-eight-states-have-that-now/>. Sarah Kliff. December 21st, 2012. "The NRA wants an 'active' mental illness database. Thirty -eight states have that now."

[256] <http://www.washingtonpost.com/blogs/wonkblog/wp/2012/12/21/the-nra-wants-an-active-mental-illness-database-thirty-eight-states-have-that-now/>. Sarah Kliff. December 21st, 2012. "The NRA wants an 'active' mental illness database. Thirty -eight states have that now."

[257] <http://overland.org.au/2012/08/when-the-burning-moment-breaks-gun-control-and-rage-massacres/>. Jeff Sparrow. August 6th, 2012. "When the burning moment breaks: gun control and rage massacres."

[258] <http://www.nytimes.com/2012/12/29/opinion/nocera-guns-and-mental-illness.html?hp&_r=1&>. Joe Nocera. December 28th, 2012. "Guns and mental Illness."

[259] <http://www.worldcrunch.com/tech-science/after-newtown-why-most-mass-murderers-are-actually-not-mentally-ill/adam-lanza-sandy-hook-killer/c4s10454/>. "After Newtown: Why most mass murderers are actually not mentally ill." December 19th, 2012. Roland Coutanceau.

[260] <http://www.usatoday.com/story/news/politics/2013/04/04/mentally-ill-gun-control-congress/2054675/>. Paul C. Barton. April 4th, 2013. "Group: Bill would ease access to guns for mentally ill."

[261] <http://www.lse.ac.uk/researchAndExpertise/units/CARR/publications/LSE-CARR-Triggeringthedebate.pdf>. Jonathon M Metzl, Kenneth MacLeish. "Triggering the debate: faulty associations between violence and mental illness underline US gun control efforts."

[262] <http://adai.uw.edu/pubs/infobriefs/ADAI-IB-2013-01.pdf>. "Alcohol, drugs, mental illness and gun violence." University of Washington. February 2013.

[263] <http://www.rand.org/blog/2013/01/can-improved-mental-health-care-prevent-gun-crimes.html>. Terry L. Schell. January 17th, 2013. "Can improved mental health care prevent gun crimes? The truth is we dont know"

[264] <http://en.wikipedia.org/wiki/Psychopath#Measurement>. Last accessed August 22nd, 2013.

[265] <http://www.ncbi.nlm.nih.gov/pubmed/14744075>. December 2003. 17(6):489-96. Maden T, Tyrer P. "Dangerous and Severe Personality disorders a new personality concept from the United Kingdom."